Essentials
of Inquiry-Based
Science, *K-8*

8 Essentials *of* Inquiry-Based Science, *K-8*

Elizabeth Hammerman

Foreword by Robert E. Yager

CORWIN PRESS
A SAGE Publications Company
Thousand Oaks, California

For information:

Corwin Press
A Sage Publications Company
2455 Teller Road
Thousand Oaks, California 91320
www.corwinpress.com

Sage Publications Ltd.
1 Oliver's Yard
55 City Road
London EC1Y 1SP
United Kingdom

Sage Publications India Pvt. Ltd.
B-42, Panchsheel Enclave
Post Box 4109
New Delhi 110 017 India

Printed in the United States of America

Library of Congress Cataloging-in-Publication Data

Hammerman, Elizabeth L.
Eight essentials of inquiry-based science, K–8 / Elizabeth Hammerman.
    p. cm.
title: 8 essentials of inquiry–based science, K–8/Elizabeth Hammerman.
Includes bibliographical references and index.
ISBN 1-4129-1498-1 (cloth) — ISBN 1-4129-1499-X (pbk.)
    1. Science—Study and teaching (Elementary) 2. Science—Study and teaching (Middle school) 3. Inquiry-based learning. I. Title: 8 essentials of inquiry-based science, K–8. II. Title.
LB1585.H27 2006
372.3'5—dc22   2005006539

This book is printed on acid-free paper.

05   06   07   08   09   10   9   8   7   6   5   4   3   2   1

Acquisitions Editor:	Jean Ward
Editorial Assistant:	Jordan Barbakow
Production Editor:	Beth A. Bernstein
Copy Editor:	Cate Huisman
Typesetter:	C&M Digitals (P) Ltd.
Proofreader:	Kris Bergstad
Indexer:	Teri Greenberg
Cover Designer:	Lisa Miller

Contents

Foreword

Elizabeth Hammerman has identified eight essentials for approaching the teaching of science as inquiry. This has been an illusive goal for most science educators in the United States for nearly 100 years. Most yearn for a more complete and accurate view of the human enterprise called science to be in evidence in classrooms in addition to the typical focus upon the major constructs that most in a given discipline accept. However, too often science is equated with the information that has amassed over time and is found in discipline-bound packages in textbooks. The assumption is made that students learn science if they can recite definitions from textbooks or repeat what they have read or remember from teachers' lectures.

Hammerman's book provides excellent research evidence to establish the importance of students experiencing science as inquiry. The reports from cognitive scientists indicate forcefully the folly of casting science only as content to be learned in classical ways. After the National Science Education Standards were published in 1996, the National Research Council sponsored the collection and analysis of the learning research and published the book *How People Learn,* a resource that is central to understanding and using inquiry. They have also published a monograph on inquiry that is larger than the 262 pages comprising the standards.

Although inquiry was basic to the major reforms of the 1960s following the Soviet exploits in space and the moves of the National Science Foundation to invest heavily in new K-12 science materials, it too often was ignored—or taken to mean a taxonomy of skills to be learned (replicated) outside of any real-world contexts. The National Standards and Hammerman's new book emphasize the importance of viewing science concepts and processes in concert with each other. In fact, the view of the whole science enterprise must be cast in even broader terms if it is to have meaning and utility for students. Such a broader view is central to the visions elaborated in the National Standards.

Science means that students will use their own questions and personal curiosity about the objects and events encountered in daily living. When these objects and events include the human mind in addition to the natural world, there is even more chance for success. Once there is curiosity there is something about the human-made world that makes every human try to do something about the curiosity which gets the brain to work. Unfortunately, these initial explanations are often wrong in terms of what scientists have come to accept as established explanations. But, the personally constructed explanations are fine in terms of religious beliefs, art, and human expressions (poems, stories, music).

The human activity called science demands more than the personally constructed explanations; evidence must be provided to establish the validity of explanations created by individuals. Doubt over the initial thinking and guesses is fundamental to science. Another feature is communicating the ideas and the evidence to others to get concurrence about which a community of scientists can agree. In terms of K-12 education, teachers and parents and students should always proceed to raise questions about whether anyone else has ever offered explanations and evidence that concur with what student groups, whole classes, or others have offered as explanations of objects and events in nature. This should appease persons concerned that students will produce "wrong" explanations if they are not given the commonly accepted ones as starting points (or corrected by the teacher, who knows the correct explanation).

Hammerman's book is rich in ideas, suggestions, and activities, all designed to energize students to do science by formulating questions, offering explanations, testing ideas, extending investigations, and communicating results. Assessment is essential to science itself; it exemplifies inquiry.

When students choose to learn, they learn basic concepts as well as the process and thinking skills needed to learn science with meaning and understanding. Science is a cyclic enterprise. Although the cycles may vary in terms of labels, the efforts mirror the total enterprise called science.

Hammerman points out that there are two conflicting features of science; namely that it is open to questioning, which also means undoing the orderliness of what we think we know and accept as a feature of the enterprise. These features by definition are missing in most classes labeled science and most textbooks chosen for study. Teachers and textbooks present science information; they do not encourage students to experience any aspect of the whole enterprise.

Hammerman's Eight Essentials illustrate well the complexities and problems with teaching science as information and skills unrelated to the lives and experiences of learners. The questions, activities, and suggestions are designed to help teachers and professional development providers with the needed changes. Such changes are critical both in the preparation of new teachers and with professional development providers who are involved with the continuing education of all teachers. Hammerman cites Iris Weiss's 2003 study of 350 lessons from a national sample of teachers where only 15% of the lessons of high school teachers and 7% of the lessons of middle school teachers could be rated highly with regard to inquiry teaching. This means that 85% of the high school teachers and 93% of the middle school teachers in the United States need experience with the eight essential features of approaching science teaching as inquiry. Hammerman's new book is designed to help resolve this most significant problem. It is a book that should be used in the nearly 1,300 institutions where science teachers are prepared and in the important task of dealing with the continuing education of all K-12 science teachers.

—Robert E. Yager
Professor of The University of Iowa Science Education

Preface

Improving Student Achievement
Through Professional Development:
A Rationale for Professional
Development in Science

Teachers are working harder than they ever have to manage class-rooms, address issues of diversity, and deliver high quality instruction, and, yet, student achievement on national assessments falls short of the high expectations we have for our nation's schools. Teacher education programs at the undergraduate level strive to provide preservice teachers with the knowledge and skills they will need to offer high quality instruction as classroom teachers. But, beginning teachers often face challenges for which they were not prepared, and the important messages from their education and methods courses are repressed as they struggle to meet the demands of the job.

Well-designed professional development initiatives can address critical needs related to standards and accountability. Quality professional development programs build on the basic foundations established in teacher education programs and take teachers to the next level of content knowledge, skill development, and confidence that empowers them to teach more effectively. The goals of high quality professional development must link closely to districtwide school improvement goals and science reform focused on increasing student achievement. Carefully crafted and managed professional development programs provide a collective focus on the vision and goals of the school system and offer multiple pathways for increasing knowledge and developing skills that lead to more effective teaching.

A recent study points to the state of the art in science and mathematics education in the nation's classrooms. In *Looking Inside the Classroom:*

A Study of K-12 Mathematics and Science Education in the United States (Weiss et al., 2003), researchers observed over 350 mathematics and science lessons and rated them on lesson design, lesson implementation, content addressed, and classroom culture. Assessment levels were assigned ranging from Level 1: ineffective instruction (passive learning and activity for activity's sake) to Level 5: exemplary instruction. Based on the observers' judgments, only 15% of the lessons were considered to be high in quality, 27% were rated medium in quality, and 59% were considered low in quality. Findings at the middle school level were even more staggering. Only 7% of the science lessons were rated high, while 78% of science lessons were rated low. Such findings send a message of importance about what teachers teach and, more important, how teachers teach.

Given that both content and methods are linked to student achievement, professional development programs must target goals to improve both the knowledge base of teachers and the skills of their discipline. Confidence and efficacy are needed to develop and maintain learning-centered environments.

References to *How People Learn* (National Research Council, 2000) and other research-based reports are made throughout this book in support of inquiry. Principles related to brain-based learning, transfer of learning, the development of thinking and problem-solving skills, and meaningful learning in general, are addressed through inquiry-based instruction. Inquiry is the process through which scientists and other professionals learn; as such, it is a powerful approach to classroom learning. This book is offered as a practical, much needed first step to addressing standards in an atmosphere of active, inquiry-based learning.

> *It is not enough to do your best; you must know what to do and THEN do your best.*
>
> —W. E. Deming

THE GOALS OF EIGHT ESSENTIALS

The Eight Essentials are designed to promote a clear, structured awareness of the ways a carefully designed inquiry-based science program can engage learners; explore natural phenomena to create a greater awareness and deeper understanding of the basic concepts and principles of science; use and develop reading, writing, and thinking skills; provide opportunities for students to reflect on and discuss experiences, frame thought and meaning through making connections and elaboration, and extend learning by developing new questions that promote further, and more open inquiry.

Eight Essentials of Inquiry-Based Science, K-8 is not a methods book, but, rather, one that focuses on inquiry-based instruction as a powerful approach to teaching key concepts and skills of science while addressing other valued learning goals. Instructional materials designed around the Eight Essentials provide teachers with the essential ingredients needed to implement high quality instruction and assessment.

Throughout this book, inquiry is shown, not as a single method, but as an approach to active learning that ranges from more structured, teacher-guided inquiry to more open, student-constructed inquiry. Many of the examples are shown in a more structured, guided discovery format to model how one might address one or more of the Essentials within an activity.

Guided inquiry questions and well-designed investigations lead the learner toward an awareness and understanding of standards-based concepts, while using and further developing process, critical thinking, and problem solving skills. A big part of the value of guided inquiry lies not only in the learning, but in the new questions that are raised throughout the learning experience. Guided inquiry also provides a teacher-friendly model of inquiry, with most samples prompting new questions and encouraging student-constructed inquiry.

USING EIGHT ESSENTIALS OF INQUIRY-BASED SCIENCE IN STUDY GROUPS AND PROFESSIONAL DEVELOPMENT INITIATIVES

The Eight Essentials offer a practical, user-friendly approach to learning about the important components of science education upon which national and state standards and assessments are based. Each chapter provides important information; sample activities; questions for discussion, reflection, and meaning making; and applications that focus on the value of inquiry-based science for meaningful learning and increased student achievement.

As a professional development resource, this book was designed to lead teachers to:

- a greater understanding of the ways that teacher-guided inquiry and student-constructed inquiry can promote the learning of important goals and standards
- an increased awareness of high quality classroom instruction

The book may be used in study groups where teachers read and study chapters on their own and come together to discuss the inquiry questions, work through the activities, and discuss classroom applications. Teachers can try new ideas and strategies by applying the Eight Essentials to their classroom instruction and discussing their experiences.

University science educators, school district science leaders, teacher leaders, school administrators, and professional development providers may use the book in more formal education programs focusing on the goals of effective teaching and learning of standards-based science.

A METACOGNITIVE APPROACH

The approach used in this book is based on a metacognitive model wherein professional development or study group participants:

- are introduced to new ideas related to inquiry
- discuss information, models, graphics, and experiences; ask questions
- interact with one another to strengthen knowledge and skills related to concepts and principles of effective teaching and learning
- extend their learning through guided or open inquiry investigations and research, as needed
- apply new learning and research-based best practices for improving student achievement
- assess the effectiveness of their instruction

This model can be replicated with students.

THE I.D.E.A. APPROACH

I Introduce

D Discuss

E Elaborate and Extend

A Apply and Assess

Introduce

Each chapter begins with an inquiry question related to the topic, which is followed by information or experiences in the form of standards, concepts, research findings, questionnaires, inventories, best practices, and activities that relate to effective teaching and learning in science. Inquiry questions are revisited to summarize learning.

Discuss

Questions that elicit thought and reflection about the topic are discussed. Through the discussion process, understandings and misconceptions are identified, beliefs and practices are challenged, action plans for learning or applying new ideas are suggested, and new questions are generated. Discussion is an important part of the process of building a greater understanding of science education and of developing confidence in the ability to teach inquiry-based science effectively.

Elaborate and Extend

Following discussion and reflection, learners may find it helpful to engage in additional activities or laboratory experiences, conduct library or Internet research, participate in field experiences, or survey or consult human and other local or state resources to elaborate on topics, answer questions, and extend or enhance learning prior to making applications to their classrooms. Here teachers may experience an "open inquiry" approach to learning by designing action plans to answer questions.

Apply and Assess

In addition to reflecting on current practices and learning new concepts and strategies, readers are encouraged to apply new learning and research-based best practices to their classroom teaching. Continuous reflection and assessment of the applications is critical for the development of new models of effective practice for future use. The form shown in Figure I.1 can be used to facilitate this reflection and assessment.

Essential #1: Inquiry-Based Science Develops an Understanding of Basic Concepts

Essential #2: Inquiry-Based Science Develops Process and Thinking Skills

Essential #3: Inquiry-Based Science Actively Engages Students in a Learning Cycle

Essential #4: Inquiry-Based Science Builds a Greater Understanding of the Ways That Science, Technology, and Society (STS) Are Linked

Essential #5: Inquiry-Based Science Provides Experiences Necessary to Support and Develop or Modify Interpretations of the World

Essential #6: Inquiry-Based Science Enhances Reading and Writing Skills

Essential #7: Inquiry-Based Science Allows for a Diversity of Strategies for Learning

Essential #8: Inquiry-Based Science Allows for a Variety of Ways for Students to Show What They Know and Are Able to Do

About the Author

 Elizabeth Hammerman is a dedicated science educator and consultant. Her professional background includes teaching science at the middle and high school levels and over 20 years of experience teaching university science education courses and codirecting funded grant projects. She has worked extensively with teachers in the field, specializing in curriculum development and implementation, performance assessment, and effective teaching and learning in science.

Elizabeth has coauthored a book on performance assessment in science and authored a database of science assessment tasks. She has published articles, presented programs at national conferences, consulted nationally, and developed curriculum and assessments for cutting-edge school districts and commercial products.

Since relocating to North Carolina in 1999, Elizabeth has been a math and science consultant for a consortium of seven county school systems; an instructional designer for SciTEC, a Web-based middle school science program; and a professional development provider and consultant for the North Carolina Department of Public Instruction.

Elizabeth is actively involved in professional development. Her books and professional development programs were designed with input from administrators and teachers who were eager to increase their knowledge, skills, and confidence for teaching science more effectively. Her *Science Achievement Professional Development Program* offers personally designed site-based program development with ongoing support for teachers in Eight Essentials of Inquiry-Based Science, Strategies for Successful Science, and Assessment as a Tool for Learning. Leadership training is offered for teacher leaders and administrators who want to offer site-based programs and to support teachers in the classroom.

Introduction

Inquiry-Based Science and the Inquiry-Based Classroom

DEFINING INQUIRY-BASED SCIENCE

Professional organizations and National Standards projects point to the importance of inquiry as the process through which students acquire knowledge and develop an understanding of and appreciation for the discipline of science.

In *Science for All Americans,* the AAAS recommends that "all students leave school with an awareness of what the scientific endeavor is and how it relates to their culture and their lives" (AAAS, 1990).

Inquiry is defined by the National Science Education Standards (National Research Council, 1996) as:

> the diverse ways that scientists study the natural world and propose explanations based on the evidence derived from their work and as the activities used by students to formulate an understanding of the work that scientists do. As a multifaceted activity-inquiry involves
>
> making observations
>
> posing questions
>
> accessing and using relevant information
>
> planning and carrying out data rich investigations
>
> using tools and technology to collect, analyze, and interpret data
>
> proposing answers, explanations, and predictions, and
>
> communicating findings

> The inquiry process fosters the use of critical thinking as well as logic and reasoning skills. (National Research Council, 1996, p. 23).

It is not enough to know science in order to teach science effectively. We know that pedagogical content knowledge is different from knowledge of general teaching methods, and that both are important for understanding how effective learning occurs in the disciplines.

> Expert teachers have a firm understanding of their respective disciplines, knowledge of the conceptual barriers that students face in learning about the discipline, and knowledge of effective strategies for working with students. Teachers' knowledge of their disciplines provides a cognitive roadmap to guide their assignments to students, to gauge student progress, and to support the questions students ask. The teachers focus on understanding rather than memorization and routine procedures to follow, and they engage student in activities that help students reflect on their own learning and understanding. (National Research Council, 2000, p. 188)

Musial and Hammerman (1992) developed a model for teaching thinking in science using the National Standards and philosophical beliefs about teaching and learning, which they applied to action research with hundreds of inservice teachers throughout the 1990s. Their work led to greater clarity of what it means to teach for understanding and to insights that support inquiry as a process for learning.

Inquiry as a Process for Learning

Learning is the dynamic process of shaping and reshaping thoughts based on new knowledge and experiences. It is the creative, ongoing synthesis of observations, reflections, and information about the physical and social worlds. The process of inquiry defines the context and processes that enable the knower to craft understanding. Inquiry is the careful, ongoing questioning of our understandings about the world around us; it is a dynamic, creative endeavor filled with wonder and surprise. These components of inquiry relate to the very heart of naturalistic knowing.

Exploring one's environment, asking theoretical and operational questions, making observations, developing hypotheses, engaging in experimentation and investigation, collecting and analyzing data, drawing conclusions, making inferences, and formulating new questions are some of the exciting processes that are practiced through inquiry-based science. Inquiry is the art of investigating questions, formulating interim answers, and, perhaps most important, critiquing potential alternative answers. Science as inquiry, then, is a social and thoughtful activity requiring much more than the practice of skills or the completion of a set of steps leading to the "right answer."

Teaching science through inquiry requires some knowledge of the ways that scientists develop questions, engage in research, and create their own frames of thought. Philosophers contend that inquiry has a bipolar character: it is anchored by two seemingly opposing forces. These are: (1) The inquiring mind is open and free. Inquiry, like the mind's nature, includes a dimension that makes us question all that is already known and understood, yet the inquiring mind has a quality of undoing and messing up the orderliness of what we know and understand. We innately have a desire to question our understanding of ideas and concepts, and experience a sense of wonder about what we don't know. (2) Inquiry is also anchored in a second dimension: the desire to shape and complete an understanding or idea. Inquiry is driven by a desire to create patterns that explain what is known. As such, there is a dimension of orderliness, structure, and finality to inquiry. This dimension of inquiry brings a sense of closure to questions, yet is challenged by the counter-dimension of wonderment.

Inquiry bridges these dualistic dimensions through the investigative process. The scientist harnesses wonderment by asking questions that lend themselves to investigation. The dimension of investigation is what connects the scientist's drive to wonder about the world to the scientist's need to shape answers and define concepts.

Dimensions to Inquiry:

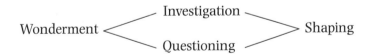

Inquiry, then, is a process of questioning within a context of wonderment, investigation, and shaping of tentative conclusions. Inquiry is the unending process of questioning and requestioning personalized understandings of the world around us.

How does this view of inquiry translate into the classroom? If teachers organize instructional experiences according to these different dimensions of inquiry, students will be more motivated and better able to develop naturalistic thinking frames.

Instruction that is patterned according to the dimensions of inquiry will:

- be rich with opportunities for students to experience and explore the world
- offer time and opportunity for students to wonder and ask questions
- permit authentic investigations wherein students develop questions; make observations; collect, record, graph, and analyze data; make sense of data, and ask new questions related to their own experiences or phenomena that affect their lives
- allow students to synthesize information, describe or create patterns, and apply their understanding to new contexts

Through the process of sharing ideas and information, new ideas and questions emerge that energize and perpetuate the cycle of learning.

TEACHING THINKING SKILLS THROUGH INQUIRY

Using an inquiry approach to instruction provides a means for addressing process and thinking skills. The nature of inquiry is rooted in the practice of using process skills and thinking strategies. Throughout all phases of inquiry, the process and thinking skills inform and assist the learner. An inquiry approach provides a natural context that enhances the acquisition of both skills and concepts. The process skills of science should be made explicit throughout the three dimensions of inquiry-based instruction. In the beginning, teachers must mediate the use of skills, redirect processes and thinking as needed, and assist students in shaping their understanding and reflecting on their skill development. The skill names should become familiar to students so that they use these words when they explain their work, reflect on what they did, and communicate findings. The metacognitive process aids in the shaping of concepts for understanding and the development of skills.

TEACHING SCIENTIFIC HABITS OF MIND THROUGH INQUIRY

Another important component of science consists of a set of dispositions or habits of mind that underlie and characterize the working scientist. Scientists seek truth about the universe by being involved in laboratory or field investigations or experimentation. Scientific behaviors that exemplify the attitudes and beliefs of scientists can be modeled by teachers and practiced by students through inquiry-based science. Dispositions such as curiosity, cooperation, honesty and integrity, open-mindedness, respect for life, willingness to suspend judgment, willingness to modify explanations, and demonstration of a respect for evidence are some examples of the habits of mind that students can practice through inquiry-based science.

Through laboratory or field investigations, students can practice safety, accuracy, good laboratory technique, systematization and organization of data, persistence, cooperation, honesty, effective communication, analysis of strategies, and replication of work. When students are able to perform in ways that scientists work, they have the best chance to develop the habits of mind that are so highly regarded by those in the field of science and in the society, in general.

Guiding and Facilitating Learning Through Inquiry

Learning in the context of inquiry requires the teacher to organize instruction according to the dimensions of inquiry. The National Science Education Standards identify five ways of guiding and facilitating learning in the context of inquiry. The standards state that teachers of science should:

- focus and support inquiries while interacting with students
- orchestrate discourse among students about scientific ideas
- challenge students to accept and share responsibility for their own learning
- recognize and respond to student diversity and encourage all students to participate fully in science learning
- encourage and model the skills of science inquiry, as well as the curiosity, openness to new ideas and data, and skepticism that characterize science

SOURCE: Reprinted with permission from National Research Council, *National Science Education Standards* (Washington, DC: National Academies Press, 1996, p.32).

Focus and support inquiries: Teachers can guide, focus, challenge, and encourage students at all levels of learning. Successful teachers are skilled observers. They match their actions to the needs of students, while deciding how and when to guide, when to challenge students, and when to provide information, tools, and resources. Effective teachers mediate the learning process by continually making decisions that help students make sense of their experiences through explanations, clarifications, examinations, and assessments of their work.

Orchestrate discourse: Oral and written discourse that focuses the attention of students on how they know what they know and how their knowledge connects to larger ideas, other domains, and the world beyond the classroom is an important part of the shaping dimension of inquiry. Teachers can directly support and guide discourse in two ways: (1) they can require students to keep accurate records of their work, and (2) they can promote different forms of communication, such as verbal, written, pictorial, graphic, electronic, or mathematical. Using a collaborative group structure, teachers encourage interdependency. Here, the teacher's role is to encourage broad participation, guide discussion, help make connections, and lead students to recognize the value of evidence and argument in an atmosphere of respect and support.

Challenge students to accept and share responsibility for their own learning: Teachers must create opportunities for students to take responsibility for their work in situations when they work individually and when they work in a group. Students should be accountable for both the processes they use during inquiry and their findings.

Teacher behaviors that encourage the development of responsibility are:

- giving students active roles in the design and implementation of investigations
- providing ways for students to be able to share their work with others
- providing tools through which students can assess the quality of their own work

Recognize and respond to diversity: Teachers need to make accommodations to provide for the diverse needs of students in their classrooms. All students should have access to equipment and be actively involved in the learning process. Some ways that teachers can monitor the learning process are by encouraging all students to ask questions and suggest answers by involving students in active learning, by modifying equipment and assignments to meet individual needs, and by encouraging diversity in the ways students communicate the results of their work.

Encourage and model the skills of scientific inquiry: By exhibiting enthusiasm and interest in the inquiry process and speaking of the beauty of scientific understanding, teachers can instill in their students similar attitudes and values. The ability of teachers to model skills of inquiry requires that they develop a knowledge of and comfort level with the content of science and with the inquiry-based teaching and learning process.

Teachers must have the opportunity to develop their own understandings and appreciation of inquiry through ongoing professional development including opportunities to work collaboratively with colleagues to share ideas, to plan instruction, to assess the effectiveness of their work, and to modify their approaches. As teachers practice the skills of inquiry through their own professional growth, they will be even more capable of modeling them in the classroom.

Implications for the Classroom

Inquiry might be thought of as the operational heart of the nature of science. It is the process that drives the scientist and determines how one interprets the world. It is through this process that concepts and principles are linked to other areas of science; to other disciplines; to technology; to the lives of students; to the community, the state, and the nation; and to the world.

The Eight Essentials of inquiry-based science address and provide further insight into each of the five ways of guiding and facilitating learning in the context of inquiry. The models and examples in the text focus on interactive instructional strategies similar to those that define the inquiry process.

Eight Essentials for Inquiry-Based Science, K-8 provides unit and lesson models that include experiences through which students can discuss their work and engage in discourse through thought-provoking questions for processing information, elaborating on findings, and creating meaning. Formative assessment tools can be used by teachers and students to provide immediate feedback, monitor learning, and develop student responsibility for learning. Opportunities for relearning or extended learning respond to diversity and allow all students to participate fully. In an atmosphere of inquiry, it is important that teachers model the skills of science inquiry, as well as the curiosity, openness to new ideas and data, and skepticism that characterize science.

If curriculum and instruction are organized around the dimensions of inquiry and if teachers develop and practice the five qualities noted in the Standards, students will be more likely to develop naturalistic ways of knowing. The implementation of this vision requires that teachers be given necessary resources, including time, materials, professional development, support, and flexibility of scheduling to enable inquiry-based teaching to occur.

Thought and Discussion

1. How does the process of inquiry relate to the natural ways that humans seek knowledge and expand their learning?

2. What are some of the barriers that impede the development of naturalistic ways of knowing in the classroom? Identify some causes for the barriers. What are some ways to overcome the barriers?

3. Design an action plan for overcoming one or more of the barriers. What are the implications for professional development related to overcoming the barriers to inquiry-based instruction?

Using the Eight Essentials as Criteria for Assessing Curriculum and Informing Instruction

The Eight Essentials provide a set of criteria for assessing high quality curricular materials necessary for implementing an inquiry-based approach to learning. As one travels through the Eight Essentials, thought and consideration might be given to curricular materials and the ways they address each Essential.

The alignment form in Figure I.1 may be used by the reader to analyze curriculum materials for the presence or absence of the Eight Essentials and comment on how they can be incorporated.

Figure I.1   Alignment of Instructional Materials With Eight Essentials

Title: _____

Inquiry-Based Science . . .	Way(s) Addressed in the Materials	Comments, Recommendations, & Suggestions
1. Develops an Understanding of Basic Concepts		
2. Develops Process & Thinking Skills		
3. Actively Engages Students in a Learning Cycle		
4. Builds Understanding of Ways That Science Is Linked to Technology & Society		
5. Provides Experience Necessary to Support & Develop or Modify Interpretations of the World		
6. Enhances Reading & Writing		
7. Allows for a Diversity of Strategies for Learning		
8. Allows for a Variety of Ways for Students to Show What They Know and Are Able to Do.		

Traditional Versus Inquiry-Based Classrooms

The behaviors of the teacher, the role of student, and the nature of the student work are three categories of beliefs and practices that define the classroom climate. In Figure I.2, indicators that characterize the traditional classroom and the inquiry-based classroom are shown for each of the three categories: Behaviors of the Teacher, Role of the Student, and Nature of the Student Work. The inventory provides a tool for identifying the degree to which each indicator relates to the inquiry-based classroom and provides a basis for discussion of beliefs and practices.

Activity

Place an X on the number that best represents the current position of your classroom with relation to each of the indicators.

Use the findings to identify one or more professional development goals that would take you closer to providing an inquiry-based classroom for your students. As you use this book, you can also return to this chart to assess development of inquiry in your teaching practice.

Figure I.2   Traditional Versus Inquiry-Based Classroom Behaviors

Traditional Classroom Teacher Behaviors	1	2	3	4	5	Inquiry Classroom Teacher Behaviors
Expository method dominates; "teach is tell" mentality; test preparation is major focus; vocabulary words are defined and memorized						Uses a variety of methods and strategies to investigate and analyze questions and address standards; communicates with students using vocabulary
Directs all activities for students; uses a cookbook—one-right-answer approach						Allows students to ask questions and design activities; mediates and monitors learning
Tells students what they will learn; demonstrates or explains the concepts and relationships						Facilitates student thinking; allows students to explain concepts; uses wait time in questioning; encourages critical and creative thinking
Uses same content every year						Learns with students; revises content and approaches based on student achievement data
Uses text and video for content and verification of concepts						Uses a variety of resources; provides a meaningful context for engaged learning
Instruction focused on "right" answers with minimal relevance or application to real world						Instruction guides students to concept and skill development and varied applications to selves, their community, and the world
Student as Passive Receiver						*Student as Active Learner*
Listens to lectures or takes notes						Records data, processes information, and builds understanding
Memorizes terms and facts						Uses terms and facts to describe, interpret, and communicate
Follows teacher or worksheet directions with no deviation; seeks right answers						Designs activities, research, and investigations to answer questions
Regards teacher as authority						Shares responsibility for learning; assesses self
Student Work—Prescribed						*Student Work—Varied*
Emphasis on definitions, notes, worksheets, or end-of-chapter questions						Emphasis on investigations, student- generated data, research, and meaning
All students complete same tasks; canned labs						Tasks vary; investigations are real-world with emphasis on data and research
Teacher directs all tasks						Teacher and students direct tasks
Shows little or no thinking or reasoning, problem solving, or explanations						Shows evidence of thinking, reasoning, problem solving, explanations, and research
Little or no use of visuals to show understanding or relationships						Uses visuals to show and describe understanding and relationships

Essential #1: Inquiry-Based Science Develops an Understanding of Basic Concepts

1

UNDERSTANDING BIG IDEAS IN THE CURRICULUM

What are some ways inquiry-based activities address the "big ideas" and concepts and principles of science? In national and state standards projects, basic concepts of science are clustered under "big ideas." Specifically, these are called *unifying concepts and processes* in the National Science Education Standards (NSES; National Research Council, 1996) and *themes* in the Benchmarks for Science Literacy (AAAS, 1993). The big ideas of science provide a structure on which knowledge can be built. They cross disciplines and provide an important mental framework for storing knowledge and showing relationships between the disciplines, a key factor for understanding.

Review the basic *themes* of the Benchmarks for Science Literacy:

- *Systems:* A complex interaction of parts that compose a whole. The term implies detailed attention to inputs and outputs or to interactions among the components of a system. The theme also refers to the ability to think about a whole in terms of its parts and to think of parts in terms of how they relate to one another.

- *Models:* Models are tentative, human created schemes or structures that correspond to real objects, systems, events, or natural phenomena. Physical, mathematical, and conceptual models are tools for learning about the objects and events they resemble, especially when the actual things are readily available or visible.

• *Constancy and Change:* Constancy refers to anything that does not change, such as symmetry or the earth's rotation and revolution. Change is a process of something becoming different over time. Much of science and math has to do with understanding how change occurs in nature and in social and technological systems. Small changes in a system at one point in time may produce very large changes later.

• *Scale:* Most variables in nature such as size, distance, weight, and temperature show immense differences. Three very important notions related to scale are the immense size of the universe, the minute size of molecules, and the age of the earth and the life on it.

The Organizational Framework for Science Curriculum in Figure 1.1 shows the way science education standards at the national, state, district, and classroom levels are linked.

Figure 1.1   Organizational Framework for Science Curriculum

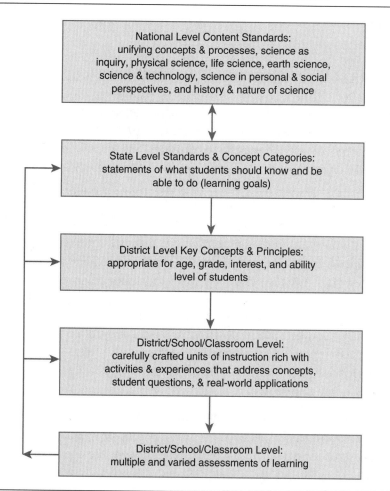

Review the *unifying concepts and processes* of the National Science Education Standards:

- *Systems, Order, and Organization:* A system is an organized group of related objects or components that form a whole. Systems have boundaries, components, resources, flow, and feedback. They are the largest collections of objects used for purposes of describing, predicting, or explaining. Order and organization may take the form of classification systems, grouping patterns, predictable sequences, or stages in a process.

- *Evidence, Models, and Explanation:* Evidence consists of observations and data on which scientific explanations are based. Models are schemes or structures that correspond to real objects, events, or classes of events, and that have explanatory power. Models take many forms, including physical objects, plans, mental constructs, mathematical equations, and computer simulations. They may change over time as new information is discovered. Explanations are logical statements that incorporate scientific knowledge and evidence obtained from observations, experiments, or models.

- *Change, Constancy, and Measurement:* Although most things are in the process of change, some properties of objects and processes are characterized by constancy, including the speed of light, the charge of an electron, or the total mass and energy in the universe. Changes occur in properties of materials, position of objects, motion, and form and function of systems. Changes in trends and cycles vary in rate, scale, and pattern. Measurement provides a quantitative method for describing constancy and change.

- *Evolution and Equilibrium:* Evolution is a series of changes, some gradual and some sporadic, that accounts for the present form and function of objects, organisms, and natural and designed systems. Equilibrium is a physical state of balance between opposing forces.

- *Form and Function:* Form and function are complementary aspects of objects, organisms, and systems in the natural and designed world. The form of an object or system is usually related to use, operation, or function.

Thought and Reflection

Review your state or district curriculum standards:

1. Are big ideas included in the documents? If so, identify them and explain how they are used to structure the content of science,

2. What are the expectations for learning with regard to the big ideas?

Thought and Discussion

An example of the relationship of big ideas to concept categories and topics in life and physical science is shown in Figure 1.2.

Figure 1.2   Topics in Elementary Science Linked to Big Ideas

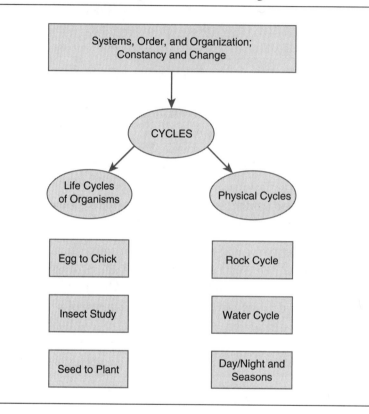

1. Discuss how each topic addresses the big idea of cycles and one or more of the others.

2. What are the common factors in the topics that allow them to be clustered under the headings?

3. What is necessary for students to be able to identify and describe the relationships between the topics?

Standards as Concept Categories

Besides addressing content standards for life, earth and space, and physical science, national and state standards address the history and nature of science, science as inquiry, science and technology, and science in personal and social perspectives. The standards documents do not always identify the contexts (topics, instructional experiences, use of resources, strategies, etc.) for learning. Those decisions are left to the curriculum developer or classroom teacher.

Figure 1.3 shows the categories of content standards for life science, earth and space science, and physical science for the early elementary and middle/upper elementary grades. These content categories are found in many state documents and science programs and provide a framework for K-8 science education.

Figure 1.3   NSES Content Standards for Life, Earth and Space, and Physical Science

Early Elementary	Middle/Upper Elementary
Properties of objects and materials	Properties and changes of properties in matter
Position and motion of objects	Motion and forces
Light, heat, electricity, and magnetism	Transfer of energy
Characteristics of organisms	Characteristics of organisms
Life cycles of organisms	Structure and function in living systems
Organisms and environments	Reproduction and heredity
Properties of earth materials	Regulation and behavior
Objects in the sky	Populations and ecosystems
Changes in Earth and sky	Diversity and adaptations of organisms
	Structure of the earth system
	Earth's history
	Earth and the solar system

Reprinted with permission from National Science Education Standards © 1996, by the National Academy of Sciences, courtesy of the National Academies Press, Washington, DC.

Thought and Discussion

Option 1: Select any one or more of the concept categories listed under early elementary or middle/upper elementary and give examples of topics that may be used to address the concept category.

Option 2: Make a list of the science topics that are taught at your grade level and classify them by content categories.

How does a list of concept categories or standards help to inform the design and development of curriculum? What are the strengths and limitations of this approach to curriculum development?

Using Standards to Inform Curriculum and Instruction

For each of the standards or concept categories there is a set of fundamental concepts and principles that provide a more accurate description of what students should know and be able to do related to that standard. Standards, along with their concepts and principles, provide direction for the development of standards-based units of instruction, since they identify what students should know and be able to do with relation to the concept category. Based on these or similar clear targets, instructional activities and experiences can be selected or designed to meet goals, thus providing an instructional program that is aligned with standards. Classroom assessments can be embedded into the instructional program to monitor and guide the learning process and to determine the degree to which goals were met.

Example #1: K-4 Earth and Space Science—Standard: *Objects in the Sky*

NSES concepts and processes:

- The sun, moon, stars, clouds, birds, and airplanes all have properties, locations, and movements that can be observed and described.
- The sun provides the light and heat necessary to maintain the temperature of the earth.

Classroom Applications for the Objects in the Sky *Standard:*

Engagement: Begin by asking students what the sun, moon, stars, clouds, birds, and airplanes have in common. Determine what students know about these objects in the sky; ask what they would like to know about objects in the sky. Identify inquiry questions and allow students to suggest ways they would like to study objects in the sky.

Exploration: Take students outdoors to make observations of clouds, birds, airplanes. Ask them to describe what these objects in the sky have in common. Describe and demonstrate motion of objects in the sky and changes in objects over time.

Figure 1.4 Activities and Assessments for Sample Units

Sample Unit Titles	Sample Activities That Address Key Concepts	Sample Assessments
A Study of Shadows	Study shadows and changes in shadow sizes and locations over time. Describe the role of the sun in creating shadows.	Describe properties of objects in the sky.
	Observe changes in light and heat in the direct sun and in shady areas throughout a day.	Describe the movements of objects in the sky.
	Gather data and describe the changes in heat on various surfaces throughout the day: blacktop, cement, soil or grass, buildings, etc.	Explain changes in shadows over time.
		Notebook entries with data and explanations about properties of objects and movements of objects.
		Data and explanations to show the effects of sunlight on the earth.
Phases of the Moon	Students may observe the changes in phases of the moon by observing it over a period of time as part of an introduction to the earth-moon-sun system.	Notebook entries and drawings of the moon over time.
		Describe properties of the moon at various phases.
		Describe changes in the moon in a month.
		Demonstrate or explain what causes these changes.
Clouds and Weather	Make observations and record movement of clouds. The formation & movement of clouds may be studied during a unit on weather.	Describe properties of clouds and their movement in the sky.
	Record differences in temperature with and without clouds.	Describe types of clouds and associated weather.
		Notebook entries.
		Describe the differences in temperature and light with and without clouds.
Birds, Insects, and Other Things That Fly	When studying birds or insects as groups of animals, observe and describe properties that make it possible for them to fly. Study feathers and wings with magnifiers and draw the structures. Note unusual features; note shapes of birds and their wings and insects and their wings.	Describe and compare objects in the sky.
	Observe flight patterns and compare flight of birds with flight of airplanes and gliders. Include concepts related to aerodynamics—gravity, lift, air pressure, and others as appropriate.	What are the unique properties of birds and insects that enable them to fly?
		How are birds and insects similar to other objects in the sky? How are birds and insects different from other objects in the sky?

Use a lesson plan format, such as the modified Five E's format (Engagement, Exploration, Explanation, Evaluation, Extension, and sometimes Elaboration) that will be modeled throughout this book, to carefully craft thoughtful, engaging experiences.

Concepts and principles can be studied through any one of a number of instructional topics. To get the most from instructional time, it is important to design and construct units of instruction that address multiple concepts and principles and standards.

Sample classroom applications with ideas for activities and assessments for concepts and principles for two content categories are shown for K-4 *Objects in the Sky* (Figure 1.4) and for K-8 *Structure of the Earth System* (Figures 1.5 and 1.6).

Example #2: Grades 5–8 Earth and Space Science—Standard: *Structure of the Earth System*

NSES concepts and processes: There are 11 concepts and processes clustered under this standard. Two of the key concepts from the *Structure of the Earth System* standard are:

- Soil consists of weathered rocks and decomposed organic material from dead plants, animals, and bacteria. Soils are often found in layers, with each having a different chemical composition and texture.
- Water, which covers the majority of the earth's surface, circulates through the crust, oceans, and atmosphere in what is known as the *water cycle*. Water evaporates from the earth's surface, rises, and cools as it moves to higher elevations, condenses as rain or snow, and falls to the surface where it collects in lakes, oceans, soil, and in rocks underground.

Classroom Applications for the
Structure of the Earth System *Standard*

The concepts for soil and water offer the teacher clues to content information and skills that will provide students with a basic understanding of these topics and enable them to build on their knowledge base. Related topics, such as landforms, and other features of the earth's crust might be dealt with separately, but, for efficiency, they may be clustered, along with important concepts, into units of instruction focusing on the lithosphere or the hydrosphere.

Figure 1.5 Activities and Assessments for a Unit on Soil Science

Sample Unit Titles	Sample Activities that Address Key Concepts	Sample Assessments
Soil Science (as part of a larger unit on the lithosphere)	Observe similarities and differences in the soils found outdoors. Observe and draw soil profiles. Take samples of soil and separate components. Observe and describe the similarities and differences in the compositions of soils. Use test kits and tools to determine pH and properties of soils from different layers. Compare soils from different areas. Use notebooks to record observations and drawings, describe activities and data, and make conclusions; record key concepts and learning.	Describe the composition of soil (organic and inorganic components). Explain and show evidence that soils in different layers have different chemical compositions and textures. Notebook entries and projects.

Soil Study

Engagement: Begin by asking students what they know about soil. What is it made of? Does soil change as you dig into the earth? Why is soil an important factor in plant growth? Identify misconceptions students have about soil and generate inquiry questions about what they would like to know. (Other creative ways might be used to engage students such as reading a letter inviting them to be a part of a team that is assembled by the U. S. Geologic Survey to investigate soils in their area.)

Exploration: Take students outdoors to make observations of soil. Use a soil sampler or dig down about a foot deep to get a cross section of soil. Record observations. Collect soil samples from a variety of locations, if possible: field, forest, stream, hillside, etcetera, for comparison. Put each sample into a small plastic bag and label with date and location.

Design a set of age-appropriate activities using samples to investigate properties, conduct tests, make comparisons, and investigate student inquiry questions.

Water Study

Engagement: Ask students what is meant by the statement: "Water, water, everywhere, but not a drop to drink." Discuss fresh versus salt water and

Figure 1.6   Activities and Assessments for a Unit on Water

Sample Unit Titles	Sample Activities that Address Key Concepts	Sample Assessments
The Wonderful World of Water (as part of a larger unit on the hydrosphere)	Use a world globe to estimate and calculate the percentage of the earth's surface that is covered by water.	Draw and explain the water cycle.
	Compare evaporation of water from open and closed containers. Observe the formation of condensation in a closed terrarium or simulated water cycle in a Baggie.	Describe the role of heat energy in the functioning of the water cycle.
	Describe factors that influence: Rates of evaporation and condensation; Types of precipitation; Movement of water on the earth; Ability of water to permeate soil and rocks.	Notebook entries related to the cycling of water through the earth and atmosphere.
	Trace the flow of water through the water cycle. Explain the process.	
	Use a notebook to record observations, activities and data, and notes and drawings; record conclusions and key concepts learned.	

determine what students know about the distribution of water on the earth. Identify misconceptions students have about water and generate inquiry questions about what they would like to know.

Exploration: Design a set of age-appropriate activities to investigate the distribution of water on the earth, properties of water, the water cycle, and the sun as the source of energy for the water cycle.

USING ACTIVITIES TO ENGAGE LEARNERS AND PROMOTE INQUIRY

This time-tested activity *How Many Drops?* is an example of one way an activity or experience can be used to introduce a concept and prompt students to ask questions about what they don't know, that is, to cause wonder and to generate questions that lead to further inquiry. The activity also provides a basis for a discussion of ways that activities can engage learners, visually display concepts, promote discussion, and lead to new questions.

Overview: The activity will address the questions: How many drops of water can the heads side of a penny hold? What property of water allows it to accumulate on a penny?

The activity introduces an important property of water, promotes discussion of variables, identifies observations and inferences, and provides the stimulus for students to ask inquiry questions about properties of water.

Materials: Per person: small cup of water; eyedropper; paper towel; penny.

Engagement

Prediction: How many drops of water will the heads side of the penny hold? I think the penny will hold ___drops of water.

Exploration

Place a paper towel on the table; place a penny on the towel. Use an eyedropper to carefully place drops of water on the heads side of the penny. Continue to add drops until the water moves off the penny. Count carefully. Conduct three tests. Record data on the chart (see Figure 1.7) and find the average number of drops for the three trials. Describe and make a drawing of your observations.

Explanation

Questions for Discussion:

1. Did everyone get the same number of drops on their pennies? Should they? If so, why do you think they were similar? If not, why do you think they were different?

2. What are variables? Were the eyedroppers the same? Did every person squeeze the bulb the same way and with the same amount of force? Were all the pennies the same?

3. How can you make comparisons among outcomes where the equipment and procedures vary?

4. Describe your observations of the water on the penny. Were you surprised at what you observed? Have you ever seen water behave the way it did in this investigation? When or where?

Figure 1.7   Data Table and Observations

How Many Drops? Data Observation Sheet

Trial #	Number of Drops
1	
2	
3	
Total:	
Average # of drops	

Drawing of Observation:

Observations:

Explanation:

5. Do you know the name of the property of water you discovered? The property is called *surface tension*. Read Paul Hewitt's definition of surface tension below and compare your observations to the definition.

> Surface tension is the contractive force of the surface of liquids.
>
> Surface tension accounts for the spherical shape of liquid drops. Raindrops, oil drops, and drops of molten metal are all spherical because their surfaces tend to contract and force each drop into the shape having the least surface. This is a sphere, for a sphere is the geometrical figure that has the least surface for a given volume.
>
> Surface tension results from the contraction of liquid surfaces which is caused by molecular attractions. Beneath the surface, each molecule is attracted in every direction by neighboring molecules, with the result that the surface of a liquid is pulled only by neighbors to each side and downward from below; there is not a pull upward. These molecular attractions tend to pull the molecule from the surface into the liquid. This tendency to pull surface molecules into the liquid causes the surface to become as small as possible. The surface behaves as if it were tightened into elastic film. Surface tension of water is greater than that of other common liquids. (Hewitt, 1989, pp. 223–224)

Elaboration

Extensions:

1. Based on your experience, how many drops of water do you think the tails side of the penny will hold? Will it be more or less than what you predicted for the heads side? Why?

2. Test other liquids, such as alcohol, soapy water, and salt water, for surface tension and compare them to tap water.

New Questions:

1. Now that you have seen what surface tension looks like, what would you like to know about this property of water?

2. Use the definition from Paul Hewitt, if necessary, to develop a set of inquiry questions about surface tension.

3. Add questions about other properties of water that you would like to investigate or research.

Evaluation

1. Write a definition for surface tension based on your experience and support it with the data you collected.

2. Identify notebook entries that show understanding of concept and reflection skills.

Teacher Analysis of the Activity

1. What characteristics does the *How Many Drops* activity have that might make it a good opener for a unit on water?

2. How does the activity address one or more of the big ideas of science?

3. How does the activity demonstrate a concept? Use the definition given from Hewitt's physics book to write a definition for surface tension for your grade level.

4. In what ways does the activity prompt questions? How can you use student-generated questions about surface tension and properties of water to inform instruction?

5. Give an example of one or more activities or experiences that you use (or have seen used) that directly address a concept or principle of science.

Revisit the Original Question

What are some ways inquiry-based activities address the big ideas and concepts and principles of science?

Essential #2: Inquiry-Based Science Develops Process and Thinking Skills

2

W hat are the ways that inquiry-based science develops process and thinking skills? The thinking skills associated with asking questions, investigating natural phenomena, solving problems, and making sense of data by formulating conclusions and structuring thought are basic to the lives of students and to the goal of developing problem-solving and decision-making skills. Within the realm of science education, a set of basic and integrated process skills has been identified as most useful. These skills are not unique to science, but help to define thinking and ways of knowing in the discipline.

SCIENCE PROCESS SKILLS

Observation: includes the use of one or more of the senses to identify properties of objects and natural phenomena. Scientific investigation begins with making observations and increasing awareness.

Classification: a system or method for arranging or distributing objects, events, or information. Classification systems range from simple to complex or multistage. Serial ordering is a type of classification where objects are distributed along a continuum from one extreme to another, such as lighter to darker (color), roughest to smoothest (texture), shortest to tallest (size), etcetera.

Making Inferences: giving explanations for an observation or drawing conclusions based on logic and reasoning; inferences, generally, follow observations for which the cause is not apparent.

Prediction: forecasting future events or conditions; predictions allow us to use what we know to extend our thinking to what we don't know. A hypothesis is a special type of prediction. In an experiment, a hypothesis predicts what the researcher thinks the relationship between the manipulated variable and the responding variable will be.

Measurement: involves making quantitative observations by comparing an object, event, or other phenomenon to a conventional or nonconventional standard.

Using Numbers: counting and creating categories; applying mathematical rules or formulae to quantities.

Creating Models: using two- or three-dimensional graphic illustrations or other multisensory representations to communicate ideas or concepts.

Defining Operationally: naming or defining objects, events, or phenomena on the basis of their functions or identified characteristics.

Identifying Variables: recognizing factors or events that are likely to change under certain conditions.

Formulating Hypotheses: making statements that are tentative and testable; a special type of prediction that suggests relationships between variables.

Recording and Interpreting Data: collecting, storing (through writing, drawing, audio or visual display, etc.), and analyzing information that has been obtained through the senses; making sense of data by determining patterns or relationships.

Drawing Conclusions: making summary statements that follow logically from data collected throughout an experience or experiences.

COMPLEX THINKING SKILLS

In addition to the process skills, there are additional skills that are particularly useful in processing data, making sense of experiences, framing thought, and communicating.

Comparing: The ability to describe objects and events by their properties and determine how things are alike and how they are different. *Venn diagrams* are often used to show comparisons.

Creating Representations: The ability to generalize a pattern of information and represent it in another way such as through the use of graphic organizers.

Making Analogies: The ability to design and describe ways that objects and events are alike (categorically or otherwise) to illustrate an understanding.

Reasoning: The ability to draw inferences or conclusions from known or assumed facts. Drawing conclusions in inquiry-based investigations develops reasoning.

Problem Solving: The ability to design and explain a possible solution or solutions when given a set of conditions or circumstances. Technological design and Science Olympiad engage students in problem solving.

Inventing: The ability to design a product or process that shows a deeper understanding or to apply a concept. Inquiry-based science provides multiple opportunities for applications.

Metacognition: The ability to reflect on one's own thinking. Carefully crafted units of instruction include questions for discussion, reflection, and meaning making.

The goals of science education include the development of skills for decision making, problem solving, and critical thinking, and the development of these must begin as early as possible in a child's life. It is critical that students learn about these important skills and appreciate them as they develop the ability to use skills throughout the learning process. Teachers should model the vocabulary of science and students should refer to specific skills as they develop and describe action plans for inquiry investigations and as they reflect and make sense of their experiences. Lists of process and thinking skills may be posted in the classroom as a reference for teachers and to students and as a reminder to use them often.

Thought and Discussion

Review the process skills:

1. Discuss the meaning of each skill and give examples of such one in the context of science.

2. Suggest one or more ways each skill can be developed in the classroom.

Revisit the *How Many Drops* activity:

1. Identify the process and thinking skills that were used in the activity.

2. What roles did the process skills play in creating a meaningful learning experience?

3. Describe how students' concept of surface tension would be different if they merely wrote the definition in their notebooks from the teacher's lecture and, perhaps, saw a picture of the phenomenon.

ACTIVITIES THAT DEVELOP SKILLS FOR LEARNING AND CONCEPT UNDERSTANDING

The sample activities are rich with process and thinking skills. They provide models for teacher-guided or student-constructed inquiry. Note the important roles of skills for engaging students, prompting rational thought, and communicating ideas and understandings.

GUIDED INQUIRY ACTIVITIES FOR THE UPPER PRIMARY AND INTERMEDIATE LEVEL: AN INTRODUCTION TO METRIC MEASUREMENT AND THE STRUCTURE OF SEEDS

Overview

Students will be introduced to the basic units of the metric system as they measure the length, volume, and mass of peanuts and investigate the structure of peanut pods and peanut seeds. Practice using the measurement tools and the units of measure in a simple context will help students become acquainted with the metric units and the relationships between them.

Students should use a notebook to record observations, measurements, etcetera from each of the six activities.

Students will study the structure and variation of seed pods and individual seeds, using peanuts.

Safety

Be aware that there may be students who are allergic to peanuts. Check health records or obtain parent permission before conducting these activities.

Instructional Objectives

The metric system is the mathematical language of science. Understanding of the basic units of the metric system comes through practice and familiarity.

Following this activity, students will:

- describe mass, length, and volume of peanuts in terms of grams, centimeters and millimeters, and milliliters
- use appropriate tools and techniques to gather, analyze, and interpret data
- use notebook data, graphs, drawings, etcetera, to explain variation within a population of organisms
- describe the structures and functions of peanut pods and of single peanut seeds
- be able to apply and use mathematics in scientific inquiry

Background Information

The U.S. Metric Association (USMA), Inc., with headquarters in Northridge, CA, is a national nonprofit organization, founded in 1916. It advocates U.S. conversion to the International System of Units, which is known by the abbreviation SI (ess-eye). SI is also called the modern metric system. The process of changing measurement units to the metric system (SI) is called metric transition or metrication.

Web sites provide an abundance of information about the metric system:

SciLinks from National Science Teachers Association: The Metric System

http://www.essex1.com/people/speer/metric.html

http://physics.nist.gov/cuu/Units/

National Institute of Standards and Technology

http://lamar.colostate.edu/~hillger/#education

Content Information

There is a great deal of variation in nature. Variation is the basis for evolution. Variation among a single population of organisms can be studied easily using peanuts. Peanuts are legumes, edible seeds enclosed in pods below the soil's surface. Peanut seeds (kernels) grow into a green oval-leafed plant about 18 inches tall. Peanuts and other legumes, such as beans and clover, allow nitrogen-fixing bacteria to live in nodules attached to their roots. These bacteria take atmospheric nitrogen (which plants cannot use) and convert it to nitrites and nitrates that can be used by plants (the nitrogen cycle). The relationship between nitrogen-fixing bacteria and peanuts is helpful to the soil because the excess nitrogen is added to the soil. George Washington Carver suggested to farmers in the early 1900s that they plant peanuts in their fields on a rotating basis with other crops in order to take advantage of the nitrogen fertilizer.

The National Peanut Board represents all U.S. peanut farmers. The board finds ways to enhance peanut production and promote the benefits of U.S.-grown peanuts. Contact them at http://www.nationalpeanut board.org/

The Peanut Institute is a nonprofit organization dedicated to expanding knowledge regarding peanuts and peanut products. A special emphasis is placed on establishing sound science as the basis for food, nutrition, and health discussions about peanuts. Contact them at http://www.peanut-institute.org/PeanutFAQs.html

Topics for Extended Learning

- the nitrogen cycle
- the life and contributions of George Washington Carver
- Peanut agriculture and uses of peanuts
- the nutritional value of peanuts

The National Peanut Research Laboratory's mission is to conduct basic and applied research to develop knowledge of the factors affecting the production, harvesting, storage, quality, and safety of peanuts. The U.S. peanut industry is in a period of economic and technological change, and research at NPRL is dedicated to maintaining and improving the competitiveness and quality of U.S. peanuts domestically and internationally. Contact them at nprl.usda.gov/Mission Statement.htm

Research is conducted to develop a better understanding of how the peanut plant copes with environmental factors, to ensure peanut safety, to develop environmentally friendly management practices, to develop equipment and technology for improving peanut market quality, and to develop a system to assess the impact of new technologies.

Materials

Per group of two students: detailed pictures of peanut plants and resources with information about peanuts or access to Internet; one metric

Figure 2.1   Basic Units in the Metric System

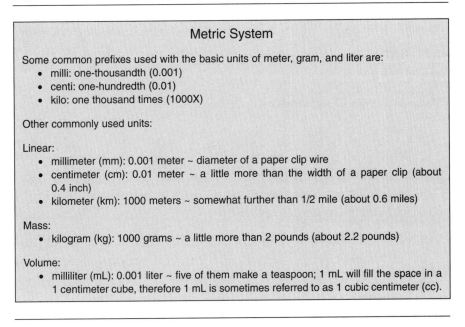

Metric System

Some common prefixes used with the basic units of meter, gram, and liter are:
- milli: one-thousandth (0.001)
- centi: one-hundredth (0.01)
- kilo: one thousand times (1000X)

Other commonly used units:

Linear:
- millimeter (mm): 0.001 meter ~ diameter of a paper clip wire
- centimeter (cm): 0.01 meter ~ a little more than the width of a paper clip (about 0.4 inch)
- kilometer (km): 1000 meters ~ somewhat further than 1/2 mile (about 0.6 miles)

Mass:
- kilogram (kg): 1000 grams ~ a little more than 2 pounds (about 2.2 pounds)

Volume:
- milliliter (mL): 0.001 liter ~ five of them make a teaspoon; 1 mL will fill the space in a 1 centimeter cube, therefore 1 mL is sometimes referred to as 1 cubic centimeter (cc).

tape measure or metric ruler; graduated cylinder; one or two magnifiers; bag of 20 peanuts in the shells; one additional peanut per person; access to balance and mass sets.

Teachers may need to design data sheets to accompany these activities or have students use notebooks for recording information.

Engagement

Ask students what they know about the metric system. Give a short pretest on metric units or hold up several objects and ask students to estimate their mass in grams, size in centimeters, or volume in milliliters or liters. Determine students' familiarity with the terminology and tools of measurement. Identify misconceptions. A short introduction to the importance of the metric system to global communication may be in order if this has not been established beforehand.

Other suggestions: Read a short scientific article that has data in metric units; identify metric units on product labels; show international weather maps with temperature data in degrees Celsius and precipitation in centimeters.

Find out what students know about peanuts. Do they know that peanuts are seeds that grow in pods beneath the soil? Allow students to discover this information as they work through the activities. However, it is helpful to identify misconceptions through initial discussion.

Give students an invitation from the National Peanut Research Laboratory asking them to assist in doing some research on peanuts to determine the degree of variation in their size, shape, mass, etcetera, using metric units.

Exploration and Explanation

Activity 1: My Peanut

1. Allow students to examine and freely explore one or more peanut pods and record questions they have about peanuts in their notebooks. Optional: Have available samples of peanuts without shells for students to taste (if allowed).

2. Give each student a peanut pod to study in detail. They should not mark them or break them in any way, but encourage attention to detail. Students should record any observations of their pod in their notebook.

3. Without telling them you will do this, collect the peanut pods in a paper bag, mix them, and pour them onto the table. Ask students to find their peanut pods.

4. Alternatively, put peanuts from three or four groups of student into small paper bags. Students then have to reach into the bag (without looking, of course) and select their peanuts by touch.

Questions for Discussion:

1. What characteristics were useful for identifying your peanut pod?

2. What characteristics of your peanut pod made it unique?

Activity 2: Dissecting a Pod

1. Have students draw their peanuts in their notebooks. Direct them to make observations of the outer covering and to label features on the drawing.

2. Are both ends similar? If not, how are they different?

3. Discuss findings and describe variation in the physical properties of peanuts.

4. Record any questions you have about the physical properties of peanuts.

5. Ask: What is the point with lines of fiber radiating from it? Introduce the term *peduncle* and have students label this part on their drawings.

Have students observe the picture of the peanut plant (see Figure 2.2). Ask students where the peanuts are located with relation to the ground. (The peanuts are located underground.) Observe where and how they are attached to the plant. What do you think the function of the peduncle was for the pod? (The peduncle is the place where the pod was attached to the plant.) Have students record the function of the peduncle and draw the peanut plant showing the attachment of peanuts.

Figure 2.2   The Peanut Plant

SOURCE: nprl.usda.gov/images/peanut%20plant.jpg

Direct students to break open the peanut pod and observe the number of seeds and note how the seeds (what we call peanuts) fit into the pod. Allow time to investigate. Then direct students to observe and dissect seeds and challenge them to find the *seed coat* made of cellulose, the edible part that is *stored food* for the seed, and the "germ" or *embryo plant.*

Now tell students to draw one seed in their notebooks and to label the seed coat, the two parts of the seed that store food, and the embryo plant.

Use a magnifier to find the tiny leaves in the embryo. Ask students what they think will happen to the small embryo (students may know this if they ever sprouted seeds and observed plant growth); what role will the leaves play in the developing plant? (Leaves contain chlorophyll for photosynthesis to occur; photosynthesis is the process by which plants make their own food.)

Have students research to find out more about each part of the pod and the seed.

Have students research some of the products that are made from peanuts, such as flour, soap, shampoo, paint, and more.

Questions for Discussion:

1. Observe peanuts that other members of your group have dissected. How are the peanuts alike? How are they different?

2. Write a statement in your notebook about how peanuts vary. Share the statements.

3. What did you discover about the structure of a seed that you did not know before?

4. What new questions do you have?

Extensions:

Give students other types of seed pods such as sugar snap peas and other types of seeds—kidney or lima beans, chick peas, etcetera, including corn kernels.

Allow students to ask questions about the seeds and investigate their questions. Allow them to dissect the pods and the seeds and observe the parts.

Discuss: Are all seeds alike? If not, how are they alike and how are they different? (Students will find that the corn kernels do not separate into two parts like the pea and bean seeds do. Further research and investigation—inquiry—will be necessary to explain this discrepancy.)

Activity 3: Serial Ordering and Measuring

1. Direct the groups to take the bag of 20 peanuts and order the peanuts by length from shortest to longest.

2. Introduce the units of centimeters (cm) and millimeters (mm) on the metric tape measures or rulers. Have students measure each peanut to the nearest millimeter and record the data for each peanut on the data table (see Table 2.1).

3. Now, measure several peanuts using centimeters. See if students can discover a relationship between centimeters and millimeters. Discuss the relationship.

4. Ask: Do you have to remeasure all the rest of the peanuts to find out their lengths in centimeters? How can you determine the number of centimeters? Convert the measurements to centimeters. Complete Table 2.1.

Table 2.1   Data Table for Linear Measurement

Peanut #	Length in Millimeters	Length in Centimeters
1		
2		
3		
4		
5		
6		
7		
8		
9		
10		
11		
12		
13		
14		
15		
16		
17		
18		
19		
20		
Mean		

5. Review of mean, median, mode.

Figure 2.3   Review of Mean, Median, Mode

Mean = Average length of peanuts in sample; add individual measurements and divide by the number of peanuts.

Median = Order the peanuts from shortest to longest. Find the length of the peanut(s) in the middle.

Mode = Find the most common length in the sample. There may be more than one mode.

---

6. Find the mean, median, and mode for the peanuts in your bag.

Mean =   **Median =**   **Mode =**

7. Find and record the means for THREE other groups. Complete data in Table 2.2.

Table 2.2   Comparing Means

Group	Mean Length in mm	Mean Length in cm

8. Make comparisons.

Figure 2.4   Bar Graph

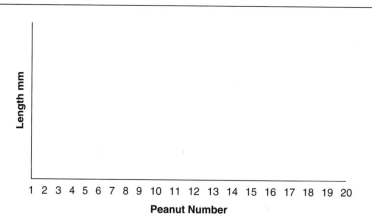

9. What is the mean length for the FOUR groups? The mean for the FOUR groups is: _____ .

   How does the group mean compare to your mean?

10. What was the range of size in your sample?

   The range of sizes extends from _____ to _____ .

Questions for Discussion:

1. Compare the mean, median, and mode for your samples. What can you say about them?

2. How would you determine the average size peanut among all the bags of peanuts used? Challenge: Find the average peanut size for all the peanuts.

3. What effect would one very large peanut in your sample have on the mean, median, mode, and range?

Activity 4: Graphing Data

1. Return to the linear measurement data. Direct students to create a bar graph to display their data. (It may be necessary to review graphing skills.)

   Complete the bar graph for the linear measurement data.

2. Direct students to create a histogram (see Figure 2.5) for their data. Review procedures, if necessary.

   Create a histogram for frequency data for the 20 peanuts

3. Have students develop a set of questions about peanuts that can be answered using their graphs. Have students share their questions and graphs with other students.

Questions for Discussion:

1. What sort of information do your graphs provide that the data table does not?

2. How would you compare your graph of length and frequency distribution with those of other groups? How are they alike? How are they different?

3. If you had another package of peanuts from the store, how do you think it would compare to the package you used? How would you test your prediction?

Activity 5: More Measurement

1. Introduce students to the balance and mass sets. Be sure students understand the basic unit they will use for the activity: gram.

Figure 2.5   Histogram

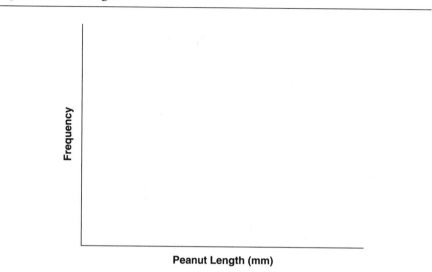

2. Ask the students what the mass (in grams) is of an average peanut pod. Predict. Record your prediction. Discuss ways to calculate mass. What will happen when you put a single peanut pod on the balance? Try it. Develop a strategy for finding the mass of one peanut and write it in the notebook. What is the mass of an average peanut pod? Have students find the average mass, make a data table, and record data.

3. Share and analyze plans, procedures, and results.

Questions for Discussion:

1. Were all the group averages the same? Would you expect a variation? Why or why not?

2. What did you learn about the mass of a single peanut pod?

3. How would you find the average mass of a single M&M candy?

Activity 6: Finding Volume

Review volume. Have students develop a plan for finding the volume of a peanut.

Evaluation for All Activities

Assess notebook entries and design formative assessments to determine if students are able to:

- describe mass, length, and volume of peanuts in terms of grams, centimeters and millimeters, and milliliters
- use appropriate tools and techniques to gather, analyze, and interpret data
- describe variation within a population of organisms
- describe the structures and functions of peanut pods and of single peanut seeds
- use mathematics in scientific inquiry

Extensions

1. Discuss how the skills helped the learners add to their knowledge base. Have students give examples of ways measurement is important in their everyday lives (sports, hobbies, dividing things, shopping, building or fixing things, cooking, assessing health-related issues, communicating, etc.).

2. Have several groups measure the same bag of peanuts to determine if they get the same measurements. Number the peanuts so that the data for each peanut can be identified and compared. What might account for differences in the measurements?

3. Discuss why it is important for student scientists to include several trials when conducting experiments or doing investigations that involve measurement of plants. (We know that there are variations among plants and there are differences in measurement techniques and tools.)

4. Allow students to develop plans for investigating questions that they recorded in their notebooks. Allow students to describe their plans, their activities, and their findings.

Thought and Discussion

1. Identify the process skills and thinking skills that were used in the measurement activities. What types of information did the measurement and thinking skills provide to the learner?

2. Although the activity was presented as a guided inquiry format, there were opportunities for students to ask questions and conduct

inquiries and research based on their questions. Identify some of the ways that students were encouraged to extend their learning.

3. How might the activity be restructured to include more student-initiated questions and investigation?

STUDENT-CONSTRUCTED OR GUIDED INQUIRY FOR THE INTERMEDIATE OR MIDDLE SCHOOL LEVEL: HEATING AND COOLING RATES OF WATER AND LAND

Overview

This activity may be part of an instructional unit dealing with properties of water (or the hydrosphere) or the properties of soil (or the lithosphere), or a unit on climate where there are questions about heat loss in water versus land. As such, it will be important for students to learn about heat loss from water and land. Two options are presented: student-constructed and guided inquiry.

Key Concepts From NSES: Transfer of Energy

Energy is a property of many substances and is associated with heat, light, electricity, mechanical motion, sound, nuclei, and the nature of a chemical. Energy is transferred in many ways.

Heat moves in predictable ways, flowing from warmer objects to cooler ones, until both reach the same temperature.

Inquiry Questions

What gains heats faster, land or water? What loses heat faster, land or water?

Prediction: I think _____ gains heat faster. I think _____ loses heat faster.

Materials

Per group of two students: two 400-milliliter beakers, 250 milliliters of sand, 250 milliliters of water, two Celsius (and/or Fahrenheit) thermometers, and a heat source—heat lamp or other.

Engagement

Find out what students know about heat. Allow them to tell what they know (identify any misconceptions) and ask questions to identify what they would like to know. Record all information and investigations in notebooks.

Exploration and Explanation,
Option 1: Student-Constructed Inquiry

Armed with the inquiry questions that address the key concepts, students may design investigations that address the questions. Students may ask additional questions as they go along, prompting the design of further investigations and research.

Students should be expected to:

- identify and record the tools and materials they will need
- design a plan for answering the inquiry questions and describe, in detail, what they will do
- record observations and show data tables
- optional: show plans to the teacher and discuss how plans will answer the inquiry questions; discuss changes or modifications needed
- conduct the investigations
- collect and record data; display data
- draw conclusions based on the data collected
- propose explanations for findings
- show data and explain findings

Suggestions

Throughout the student directed-inquiry, teachers should make observations to ensure students are on task and on track as they design their plans. Allow students to formulate ideas before discussing their strategies, but allow students to ask questions and get help, as needed, especially if they are new to the design process.

When students are required to show their plans, they have to verbalize their ideas; teachers can give approval to the processes or make decisions about whether students should be able to proceed, if plans are not suitable for answering inquiry questions.

Throughout the investigative process, teachers should be observing students' behaviors for safety and their ability to work well and accurately in a group setting. Frequent interactions with working groups offer teachers the opportunity to ask questions, enabling students to think about and communicate their procedures and share their findings as they go through the investigation.

Teachers may need to offer suggestions for improving or modifying the investigative process, but changes should be made only if students see the relevance of the suggestions or if they are a matter of improving safety.

When this activity is conducted as an inquiry, teachers—or teachers with student assistance—need to develop a set of debriefing questions for discussion, similar to those presented at the end of the next section. The set of questions will provide information to teachers and students about the effectiveness of their procedures and the accuracy of their findings. In addition to processing information, students should identify new questions they have.

During the information processing or debriefing session, discrepancies in data sets and misconceptions are identified and dealt with through relearning opportunities or additional investigations and research.

Questions should also address the meaning behind the findings. What is the significance of the relationships that were discovered? Connections should be made between the phenomena and their implications in the natural world. For example, "How do the findings affect the temperature of cities located near large bodies of water?"

Exploration and Explanation, Option 2: Guided Inquiry

1. Fill one beaker with 250 milliliters of sand or soil. Fill another beaker with 250 milliliters of water. Allow both to be at room temperature.

2. Attach a thermometer to each beaker. Make sure that the bulb of the thermometer is the same distance below the surface for both the sand and the water. For the sample data (in this case), the bulb of the thermometer was about 2.5 centimeters (1 inch) below the surfaces of water and sand.

3. Read the temperature and record it on the data table.

4. Place each beaker under the heat source and take readings in each beaker every five minutes for 30 minutes, for a total of six data entries. Record the temperatures on the data table.

5. After 30 minutes, take the beakers away from the heat source. Record the temperatures every five minutes for another 30 minutes. Record the temperatures on the data table, for a total of six more data entries. (In science experiments, data should be recorded in degrees Celsius. However, in some cases, students may only have thermometers that record degrees Fahrenheit. Both scales are given here).

6. Graph your data.

Table 2.3   Data for Heating and Cooling

Data for Heating					Data for Cooling				
	Sand		Water			Sand		Water	
Time	°C	°F	°C	°F	Time	°C	°F	°C	°F
0 min					30 min				
5 min					35 min				
10 min					40 min				
15 min					45 min				
20 min					50 min				
25 min					55 min				
30 min					60 min				

Table 2.4   Sample Data For Heating and Cooling

Data for Heating					Data for Cooling				
	Sand		Water			Sand		Water	
Time	°C	°F	°C	°F	Time	°C	°F	°C	°F
0 min	23	74	23	74	30 min	41	104	36	96
5 min	28	82	28	82	35 min	40	103	34	95
10 min	31	88	30	86	40 min	37	98	33.5	92
15 min	33.5	92	31	88	45 min	35	95	32	90
20 min	36	96	33.5	92	50 min	33.5	92	31	88
25 min	38	100	34.5	94	55 min	32	90	30	87
30 min	41	104	36	96	60 min	30	87	30	86

Questions for Discussion:

1. In the first 30 minutes, how many degrees Celsius did the sand increase? (+19 degrees)

2. How many degrees Celsius did the water increase? (+13 degrees)

3. What conclusion can be drawn about the ability of sand and water to gain heat? (Sand gains heat faster than water—or water gains heat more slowly than sand)

4. In the second 30 minutes, how many degrees Celsius did the sand decrease? (–11 degrees)

5. How many degrees Celsius did the water decrease? (–6 degrees)

Figure 2.6   Graph For Heating and Cooling

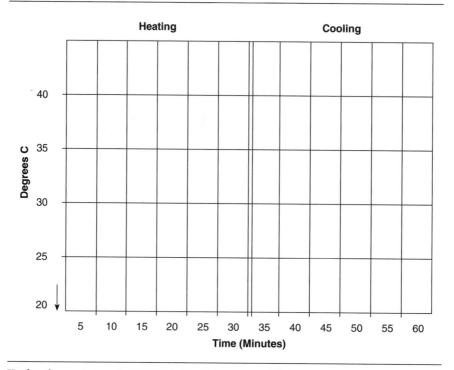

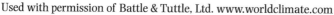

Used with permission of Battle & Tuttle, Ltd. www.worldclimate.com

6. What conclusion can be drawn about the ability of sand and water to lose heat? (Sand loses heat faster than water—or water loses heat more slowly than sand.)

7. From this simple experiment, what can you infer about how larger bodies of water gain and lose heat? (A logical inference would be that large bodies of water take a long time to gain heat, and a long time to lose heat. Water gains heat more slowly than sand, and loses heat more slowly than sand.)

8. Large bodies of water and warm ocean currents can affect climates of the land with which they come in contact. Based on what you just learned, can you explain how this might happen?

Evaluation

Evidence of student learning related to the transfer of heat energy and heat loss from water and land (the focus of the inquiry questions), along with other objectives related to skills and dispositions, can be obtained through a variety of sources. For example, notebook entries, including data tables, graphs, and explanations; checklists identifying ability to work in a laboratory setting, ability to work with others cooperatively, respect for equipment, etcetera; and performance assessments where students describe the results of their investigations are just some of the ways to gather evidence of students' learning of concepts, skills, and dispositions.

GUIDED INQUIRY ACTIVITY FOR THE INTERMEDIATE OR MIDDLE SCHOOL LEVEL: CREATING CLIMAGRAPHS

This activity is offered to show an example of the integration of science with mathematics and the use of graphs to display more than one data set. The activity also demonstrates how computer-generated (or real-time) data can be used to enhance learning. The activity is also an extension of the previous activity where the principles of heat gain and loss from water and land are applied to climate and shown to be an influence on the climate of a city.

Key Concept From NSES

Global patterns of atmospheric movement influence local weather. Oceans have a major effect on climate, because water in the oceans holds a large amount of heat.

Overview

In this activity, students will apply the principles of heat gain and loss in water to the study of climate. They will learn to construct a climagraph for two cities of similar latitude, with different geographic features. One city is located near an ocean while the other is inland. From their observations, students might infer that the ocean has an effect on the climate of the nearby city. New questions should arise about factors affecting climate for students to investigate.

Climagraphs are special types of graphs that display both temperature and rainfall data for a year. A bar graph is used to show the monthly precipitation and a line graph is used to show monthly temperatures. By observing both types of data on the same graph, climatic patterns for a geographic area can be identified.

Objectives

Students will create climagraphs using monthly temperature and rainfall data for two cities that have approximately the same latitude, but different geographic locations.

They will analyze the climagraphs and describe the relationships between the temperature and rainfall at various times of the year. They will make inferences about how geographic and geologic factors influence the average temperatures of the cities.

Materials

Graph paper; pencils

Background

Cities located at approximately the same latitude can have significantly different climates. Factors such as altitude, proximity to the ocean, wind patterns, and the like, affect climates.

Patterns of rainfall and temperature for a year provide clues about the climates. Temperature and rainfall data are collected at various locations around the world. The data show trends and patterns in temperature and amounts of precipitation from month to month and year to year. From these data, the average temperature and rainfall for a year can be calculated and seasonal patterns can be identified.

A climagraph is used to show both temperature and rainfall on the same graph. The two graphs are created with the line graph showing changes in temperature from month to month and the bar graph showing the average precipitation for each month. Temperature and rainfall data are commonly shown in degrees Fahrenheit and inches.

Creating the Graph

Mark the vertical axis on the left side of the graph in increments of five (if boxes on graph paper are small) or 10 degrees Fahrenheit, beginning with −20 degrees (or whatever temperature range fits your data). On the right side, mark the vertical axis in inches (or half-inch intervals if boxes are small). Note: Sometimes climagraphs are shown with precipitation markings on the left and temperature on the right.

The horizontal axis should be labeled with months, beginning with January. Figure 2.7 shows a data table with the temperature in degrees Fahrenheit and rainfall in inches for Buffalo, New York. Figure 2.8 shows the climagraph for Buffalo using these data.

Engagement

Discuss what information about temperature and rainfall is important for the area in which you live. If someone were to come to visit you and want to engage in a particular sport (golf, swim, ski, snowboard, hang glide, etc.), how would temperature and rainfall determine when they

Figure 2.7   Temperature and Rainfall in Buffalo

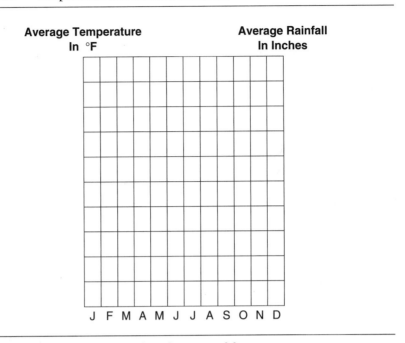

Used with permission of Battle & Tuttle, Ltd. www.worlclimate.com.

Figure 2.8   Climagraph for Buffalo

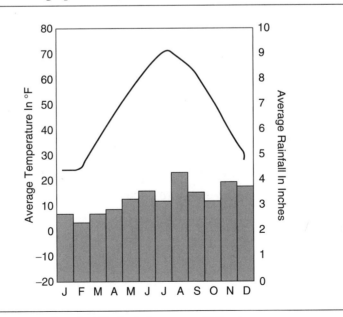

Used with permission of Battle & Tuttle, Ltd. www.worldclimate.com

should come? Are there any geologic features that affect the temperatures or amount of rainfall in your area?

What particular weather patterns are common in your area? Do you have seasons? Describe and discuss what you know. What questions do you have about climate?

Exploration

A climagraph is a special type of graph that is used to show both temperature and rainfall on the same graph.

1. The vertical axis on the left side is marked in increments of temperature in degrees Fahrenheit for showing average monthly temperature.

2. On the right side, the vertical axis is marked in inches for showing average monthly rainfall.

3. The horizontal axis is marked in months, beginning with January and ending with December.

4. A bar graph is used to show amount of rainfall; a line graph is used to show temperature changes from January to December for one year.

5. Study the sample (Figure 2.8) for Buffalo, New York (latitude 42° north; longitude 78° west). Compare the patterns on the clima-graph with the temperature and rainfall data. What seasonal patterns do you see? In what part of the United States would you expect to see Buffalo? What is the relationship (generally) between latitude and temperature? Find the city on a map of the United States. Describe the geographic location of the city and the geologic features around it. Do you see anything that might influence the temperature or amount of rainfall for the area?

6. San Francisco, California, and Lexington, Kentucky, are located at approximately the same latitude. Find the two cities on a map. Compare locations. What geologic features are located near these cities? How are they similar in location; how are they different?

Predict

How might the geographic locations of the two cities affect their climates?

Make a climagraph for each of the two cities using the information given on the data tables (see Figures 2.9, 2.10, 2.11 & 2.12) for average monthly temperature and rainfall. Most weather data in the United States are still given in inches and degrees Fahrenheit.

Make a line graph to show temperature in degrees Fahrenheit and a bar graph to show rainfall in inches for each city. Be sure to label the graphs completely.

Sample #1: Weather station SAN FRANCISCO, SAN FRANCISCO COUNTY is at about 37.76° north, 122.43° west, 72 feet above sea level (www .worldclimate.com).

Figure 2.9   Average Temperature for San Francisco, CA

	Jan	Feb	Mar	Apr	May	Jun	Jul	Aug	Sep	Oct	Nov	Dec	Year
°C	10.6	12.4	12.7	13.3	13.6	14.6	15.0	15.6	16.8	16.6	14.0	10.9	13.8
°F	51.1	54.3	54.9	55.9	56.5	58.3	59.0	60.1	62.2	61.9	57.2	51.6	56.8

Used with permission of Battle & Tuttle, Ltd. www.worldclimate.com

Figure 2.10   Average Rainfall for San Francisco, CA

	Jan	Feb	Mar	Apr	May	Jun	Jul	Aug	Sep	Oct	Nov	Dec	Year
mm	111.9	77.4	77.9	34.2	10.1	4.0	0.6	1.7	6.6	28.3	72.8	90.8	517.2
inches	4.4	3.0	3.1	1.3	0.4	0.2	0.0	0.1	0.3	1.1	2.9	3.6	20.4

Used with permission of Battle & Tuttle, Ltd. www.worldclimate.com

Sample #2: Weather station LEXINGTON BLUEGRASS, FAYETTE COUNTY is at about 38.03° north, 84.60° west, 967 feet above sea level. (www .worldclimate.com.)

Figure 2.11   Average Temperature for Lexington, KY

	Jan	Feb	Mar	Apr	May	Jun	Jul	Aug	Sep	Oct	Nov	Dec	Year
°C	−0.6	1.3	7.3	12.6	17.7	22.3	24.3	23.7	20.1	13.7	7.7	2.1	12.7
°F	30.9	34.3	45.1	54.7	63.9	72.1	75.7	74.7	68.2	56.7	45.9	35.8	54.9

Used with permission of Battle & Tuttle, Ltd. www.worldclimate.com

Figure 2.12 Average Rainfall for Lexington, Kentucky

	Jan	Feb	Mar	Apr	May	Jun	Jul	Aug	Sep	Oct	Nov	Dec	Year
mm	90.4	83.3	111.5	95.4	114.0	105.0	120.6	96.0	79.0	63.0	88.4	96.5	1144.2
inches	3.6	3.3	4.4	3.8	4.5	4.1	4.7	3.8	3.1	2.5	3.5	3.8	45.0

Used with permission of Battle & Tuttle, Ltd. www.worldclimate.com

Figure 2.13 Grids for Climagraphs

Climagraphs for San Francisco, CA
37.76° N 122.43° W

Climagraphs for Lexington, KY
38.03° N 84.60° W

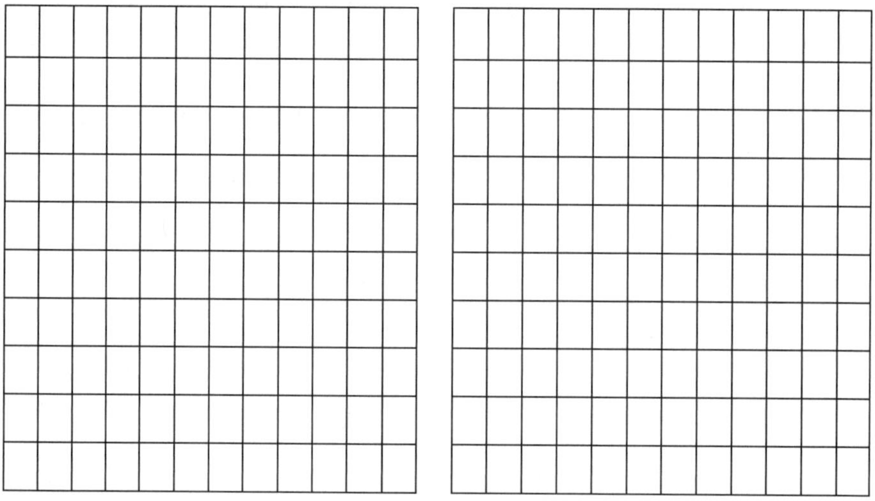

Explanation

1. The two cities have similar average yearly temperatures. Describe the differences in the temperature patterns. What might account for the differences in the patterns?

2. The amount of rainfall for the two cities is very different. What are some factors that may account for the difference in the amount of rainfall? Research geographic and geologic factors that affect rainfall.

3. Which of these climate types best describes San Francisco and Lexington?

- moist tropical climates: high temperature year round; large amount of rainfall
- dry climates: little rainfall; high daily temperatures
- humid middle latitude climates: warm, dry summers; cool, wet winters; influenced by land-water differences
- continental climates: moderate to low rainfall; moderate, seasonal temperatures with wide variation; found in interior regions of large land masses
- cold climates: permanent ice and tundra; low temperatures; only four months annually above freezing

Elaboration and Extension

1. Locate cities outside of the United States that have about the same latitude as San Francisco and Lexington. Compare average temperatures and amounts of rainfall. Identify geographic and geologic factors affecting the climates of these other cities. Make comparisons.

2. Research the temperature and rainfall data for a city close to where you live. Make a climagraph for those data. Describe the temperature and rainfall patterns shown on the graph. How do geographic and geologic features affect the climate of your area?

3. If you were to go on a vacation trip to another part of the country or the world at a particular time of the year, what factors related to temperature and rainfall would you want to know? Why would these factors be important?

Evaluation

Summarize the connections between the key concept and the instructional activity.

Key Concept From NSES

Global patterns of atmospheric movement influence local weather. Oceans have a major effect on climate, because water in the oceans holds a large amount of heat.

In what way(s) did the activity address and help students to understand the key concept?

What additional experiences might provide a greater depth of understanding of this concept?

How did the activity go beyond addressing the key concept?

Thought and Discussion

- In what ways did the activity address process and complex thinking skills?
- How did the visuals help students with identifying patterns and analyzing data?
- How did the activity integrate curriculum?
- What are some other extensions that might be included?
- How might research and new questions be used to tier instruction?

USING VISUAL ORGANIZERS TO SHOW CONNECTIONS

Visual organizers can be used by students to structure thought into meaningful patterns and show relationships among concepts. They organize thought and represent the student's way of knowing the relationships among the concepts displayed in the visual. Graphs are just one of many ways that information can be framed.

There are at least six other major structures, along with an assortment of variations, that can be used to show relationships among concepts. These structures identify descriptive, sequential, process/causal, categorical, comparison/relational, and problem/solution relationships. For example, descriptive maps are commonly used to show concepts and their characteristics or units and subunits. Figure 2.14 shows a descriptive map for the key concepts for a unit of instruction on Properties of Water. Using the graphic, students can focus on key concepts as they engage in activities related to each of them. They can see relationships between concepts and be challenged to create new visuals for each of the key concepts to describe or illustrate their understanding of them.

Another common visual organizer is a Venn diagram. This visual is used to show similarities and differences between two or more things. In Figure 2.15 the Venn diagram shows some ways that two types of animals that fly are alike and different.

Figure 2.14 Descriptive Map for Properties of Water

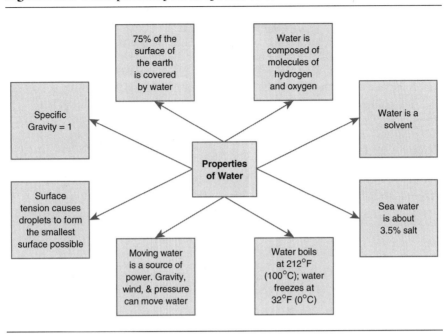

Figure 2.15 Comparison of Bats and Blue Jays

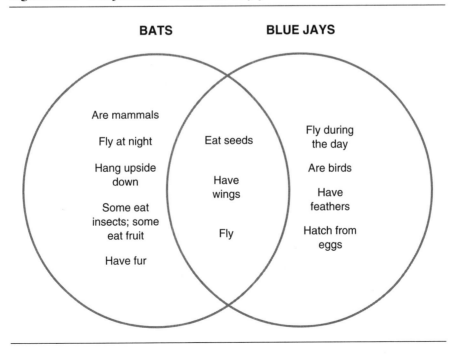

Thought and Discussion

1. How do visuals, such as graphs, Venn diagrams, or descriptive maps show thinking or the ways that students understand relationships?

2. Give an example of a visual organizer that you use or have seen and explain the relationships among concepts shown in the visual.

Revisit the Initial Question

What are some of the ways that inquiry-based science develops process and thinking skills?

Essential #3: Inquiry-Based Science Actively Engages Students in a Learning Cycle

3

How does the use of a learning cycle model help to promote meaningful learning? When students investigate, they take ownership for problems and questions that motivate them and focus on learning. Students develop plans for solving problems and answering questions and use the knowledge and skills of science to gather information that supports their conclusions. By communicating results of their investigations, students take pride in their accomplishments, link science to other subjects, discuss implications, develop confidence in their learning, and ask new questions.

Many learning cycle models have been designed and used in science education over the years. Most of the models focus on the cognitive development of the learner and the formation of patterns of thought and reasoning resulting from reflection on their involvement in science investigations. The Karplus model, on which the Science Curriculum Improvement Study of the 1970s was based, consisted of three phases: exploration, conceptual invention, and application. Educational materials offered by the AIMS Education Foundation are developed around a four-phase model for learning: doing, writing, illustrating, and thinking (AIMS, 1987, 1993). Other curricular materials and programs offer models that include these and other phases, such as identifying misunderstandings or naive ideas about topics, selecting appropriate predetermined sets of activities and experiences, and establishing new mental schemes. All models

Figure 3.1   A Learning Cycle Model

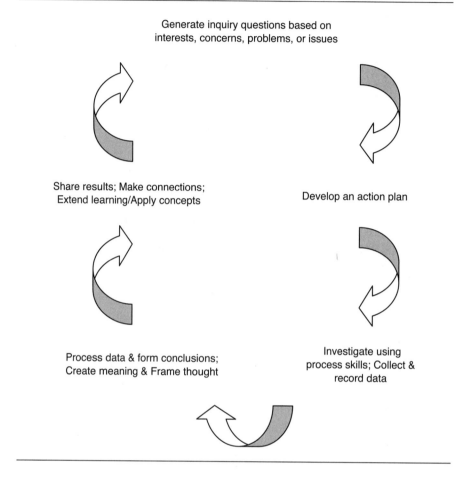

include the involvement of students in doing science and the processing of thought.

To be an inquiry model, the process should focus on questions that are of interest to students and that capitalize on the component of wonderment that we want to encourage in students. Approaches that begin by telling students what they will learn diminish the sense of wonderment and take away the "aha" or sense of discovery that may result from the observation of unexpected phenomena or results.

The learning cycle model in Figure 3.1 is a sample action plan. It highlights key questions, either generated by students from previous activities or interest, or initiated by teachers to capture student interest in a standards-related concept. Following the identification of inquiry questions, students—or students and teachers—devise a workable plan for investigating the question, with ample time allotted for investigation and collecting and recording data. A careful, thoughtful process is critical for successful inquiry, and a learning cycle model provides a starting point for this planning.

Three of the criteria that were used in the 2003 *Study of K-12 Mathematics and Science Education in the United States* (Horizon Research, 2003) to distinguish effective lessons from ineffective lessons were:

The teacher . . .

- engaged students with math or science content
- used questions to monitor and promote understanding
- helped students to make sense of the math or science content

These three factors related to high quality instruction cannot be overlooked, as research confirms their importance for learning and retention.

Research

1. Studies conducted by Hermann Ebbinghaus on memory in the late 1980s produced the *forgetting curve* that showed that approximately 70% of learned material that has no previous association or meaning for the student is forgotten within three days (Wolfe, 2001).

2. Robert Sylwester (1995) describes context and emotion as key factors influencing memory: "A memory is a neural representation of an object or event that occurs in a specific context, and emotionally important contexts can create powerful memories. When objects and events are registered by several senses, they can be stored in several interrelated memory networks. A memory stored in this way becomes more accessible and powerful than a memory stored in just one sensory area, because each sensory memory checks and extends the other" (p. 96).

3. Eric Jensen (1998) reports on the work of researchers who believe that memory and retrieval are inseparable. "Memory is determined by what kind of retrieval process is activated. The number one way to elicit or trigger recall is by association" (p. 102).

4. Patricia Wolfe (2001) supports Jensen's notion. "One of the most effective ways to make information meaningful is to associate or compare the new concept with a known concept, to hook the unfamiliar with something familiar" (p. 104).

Every attempt must be made, then, to engage students in learning and to make learning meaningful in order for them to store information and improve their ability to recall it. The data processing/reflective thinking phase may be the most important component of the learning cycle since this is the point at which meaning is created in the mind of the learner.

When students make applications of the concepts and principles to their lives, their communities, their state, their country, and other disciplines, they are not only clarifying the meaning of the content, but they are reframing thought by building on their prior knowledge. It is during this phase of thought and reflection that students identify links between the concepts they are learning and the standards and big ideas. The connections allow them to communicate, with greater clarity and elaboration, their deeper understandings.

As students share results of investigations and discuss meaning, they may experience the phase of wonderment through new questions. Questions may be theoretical, in which case they may be answered through research and additional experiences, or they may be operational; these take the student through the journey around the learning cycle once again. The learning cycle, then, is a powerful tool to be used in curriculum design and delivery as it informs and guides the developer and teacher.

Another tool that can be used to guide high quality instruction is the lesson plan. An organized and well-developed plan not only includes the important components of high quality instruction that address important concepts and skills, but it includes information that enables teachers to process data effectively, identify misconceptions, extend learning, make connections to technology and social issues, and frame thought. A format for effective lesson planning and delivery modified from Bybee (2002) is used with some variation throughout this book.

THE FIVE E'S LESSON PLAN

The Five E's lesson plan format provides a framework for classroom instruction that follows the important components of the learning cycle model. The lesson plan allows for thought and detail and includes components that:

- link concepts to standards
- identify instructional goals
- provide an overview of the investigation and key concepts
- provide background and content information
- list resources and materials that will be used
- clearly describe procedures, including the use of notebooks and graphic organizers
- describe or show data tables, graphs, charts, etcetera.
- include a set of questions for processing and meaning making

- identify ways to extend and apply learning
- identify strategies for assessment

The Five E's lesson plan format is much more than an outline of a classroom activity; it is much more than a set of phrases indicating what topic will be addressed. A well-designed lesson includes a detailed description of a complete learning experience that may be the focus for one day or several days. Thoughtful planning guides effective teaching. The lesson plan provides a format for teachers to follow as they develop the skills and confidence to teach standards-based science through teacher-guided inquiry or student-constructed inquiry.

PROCEDURES BASED ON THE FIVE E'S

Engagement (Activating and Engaging; Identifying Misconceptions)

Consideration should be given to creating a meaningful context to motivate students to investigate and apply skills and concepts. Some ways to enhance interest and promote wonder are:

- Ask students what they know and would like to know about a topic, concept, or issue. This approach will help to identify misconceptions students have and allow students to ask questions around which further investigation and research can be structured.
- Give students something to investigate and wonder about—an activity, an experience, an event, a field trip.
- Read an article about a science-related issue pertinent to the lives of students or to their community and find out what students know and would like to know about it.
- Use a discrepant event to raise questions.
- Read a letter, memo, or invitation from someone of importance to elicit student help with a project or an experiment.
- Ask students to design an action plan for gathering information about an important topic.

Exploration (Discovery Phase)

- Identify an inquiry question or allow students to identify inquiry questions. What will students DO?
- Describe procedures for guided inquiry clearly and accurately or establish a set of guidelines (if appropriate) for student-constructed inquiries.

- Process and thinking skill vocabulary words should be used throughout.
- Describe what data and information students will collect.
- Provide action plans and data tables or challenge students to design action plans and data tables. Notebook entries should be part of the procedures.

Explanation (Processing for Meaning)

- Design a set of thought-provoking questions that allow *students* to explain what they did and what they learned.
- Ask questions that allow students to build on prior knowledge and develop expanded frames of thought. Use good questioning strategies such as "wait time" and show respect for student comments and questions.
- Use student-generated data to support new learning.
- Identify discrepancies and possible misconceptions. Create meaning through reflection and discussion.

Elaboration and Extension (Making Connections)

- Include opportunities to learn more or make needed clarifications (possibly based on new questions that arise) through further investigation or research.
- Allow opportunities for students to ask new questions and engage in further investigation and research to extend learning.

The lesson becomes meaningful to students when applications are made to their lives and interests. Connections and applications should be made to technology and to society, including personal, family, community, state, national, or global issues.

Evaluation (Shaping Understanding)

How did the new learning expand or change the student's original understanding, "frame," or mental construct?

- Have students show and explain learning through reflective writing, graphic organizers, applications of knowledge, presentations, and sharing ideas and insight.
- Use formative assessment strategies to provide evidence of learning throughout the learning experience.

Modified from Rodger W. Bybee, *Learning Science and the Science of Learning* (Alexandria, VA: National Science Teachers Association Press, 2002)

Similar research-based models have been developed, including a 7 E's lesson plan by Arthur Eisenkraft (2003), Project Director of Active Physics, that gives additional attention to the eliciting of prior knowledge and the transfer of learning. Models may be modified and adapted to fit the approach teachers will use–teacher-guided inquiry or student-constructed inquiry–but it is important that all components of the model are addressed in some way in lessons to increase the likelihood that high quality instruction will occur and promote greater student achievement.

GUIDED INQUIRY LESSONS USING A FIVE E'S FORMAT: PRIMARY LEVEL—THE EAR AND HEARING

Learners will investigate the sounds that are produced from a number of different objects. They will realize that hearing is the function of the ear. Students will explore what creates sound and observe that objects vibrate when they produce sound.

Instructional objectives: Upon completion of this activity, the learner will be able to:

1. demonstrate ways that objects can produce sound

2. show that different objects produce different sounds and identify objects by their sound

3. describe the function of the ear as the organ of hearing

4. describe that objects vibrate when they produce sound

Key Concepts From NSES

The behavior of individual organisms is influenced by internal cues (such as hunger) and by external cues (such as a change in the environment). Humans and other organisms have senses that help them detect internal and external cues.

Humans depend on their natural and constructed environments. Humans change environments in ways that can be either beneficial or detrimental for themselves and other organisms.

Materials

For the teacher: rubber bands; objects that make noise or a recording of noises.

Per group of two students: various sizes of rubber bands; playing card with a hole in the center; unsharpened pencil with an eraser; two emery boards; strip of newspaper; plastic comb; plastic spoon; four-by-six-inch piece of waxed paper.

Optional (for extensions): six jars, beakers, or glasses of similar size; water; magnifiers; an assortment of old and new pennies.

Resources

Moncure, J. B. (1990). *The five senses,* Elgin, IL: The Child's World.

Moncure, J. B. (1990). *Life cycles,* Elgin, IL: The Child's World.

Gossett, C. S., et al. (2000). *Sense-able science.* Fresno, CA: AIMS Education Foundation.

Engagement

- Ask students what they think sound is. How are sounds produced?
- Have students close their eyes. Make a series of sounds for students to identify. Examples could include piano playing, whistling, singing, shouting, clapping hands, snapping fingers, etcetera. For ease of use, consider recording these sounds on a cassette tape. Help students generate a list of words used to describe the different sounds they experience. Sound words might include: loud, soft, ringing, sliding, whistling, etcetera.
- Ask students how they receive sound. Have students cover the opening to their ears. Observe again. Can they hear the sounds as well? Discuss.
- Have students identify the sounds and describe the function of the ear as the organ of hearing.

Exploration

- Individually or in small groups, have students arrange the materials listed above on the table in front of them.
- Instruct them to look, but not to touch the objects until directed to do so. Hold up each object and ask the students to predict which objects will be able to make sounds and which will not. Record predictions.
- Give each pair of students a rubber band and allow one student to hold the rubber band while the other plucks it to produce sound. Varying the sizes of the rubber bands will allow students to observe and compare the sounds produced. Challenge students to try to hum the sounds they hear.
- Ask students if they can use a pencil to produce sound. Have students pick up their pencils and demonstrate using the wooden

end (students can experiment with sound by tapping pencils on the desk, floor, chair, etc.). Have them repeat the process using the eraser end of the pencil. How is the sound produced with the eraser end different from the sound produced with the wooden end?

- Rub and tap the emery boards.
- Tap and snap the playing card; blow through the hole in the playing card.
- Wave and tear the newspaper.
- Tap and flip the plastic spoon.
- Tap the comb and feel the vibrations as students move the teeth of the comb against the table.
- Discuss what students did to produce sound.
- Have students strike the rubber band again and feel it. Are they able to sense the vibrations made when sound is produced?
- Repeat some activities, asking students to sense vibrations.
- Research what causes sound. Use reference books such as *How Science Works* (Hann, 1991) or read stories about sound, such as *The Other Way to Listen* (Baylor, 1978) and *The Very Quiet Cricket* (Carle, 1993).

Explanation

Questions for Discussion
- Ask students to describe how the things they tested vibrated to produce sound.
- Discuss ways that the sense of hearing is helpful to humans (alerts humans to danger; allows them to appreciate and enjoy pleasant sounds such as music and the sounds of nature; allows humans to communicate with one another).
- Is the sense of hearing ever harmful to humans (when sound is too loud, it can be damaging to the eardrum as with explosions or loud music; when there is noise that prevents humans from concentrating on something that is beneficial to them)?
- What are some ways that humans change their environment to make it beneficial to them or harmful to them?

Elaboration

Application 1
1. Introduce the big idea of system (putting two or more things together to accomplish a task) by showing students how to make a sound system. Fold waxed paper over the teeth of the comb. Have

students make a humming sound by putting their lips together. Hum a tune such as "Old MacDonald Had a Farm."

2. Have them put their fingers to their throat while humming and feel the vibration of the sound. What is vibrating? If possible, have a picture of vocal cords. Demonstrate holding the comb-harmonica system loosely between the lips and have students hum a song on their comb-harmonica. Have students experiment with different hums.

3. Have them feel the vibration of their vocal cords.

4. Ask what is vibrating.

Application 2

Making music:

1. Have students pick their favorite object from the materials in front of them and hold it in the air.

2. Set a beat and have them join in to make music with their objects.

Evaluation

1. What part of the body do we use to hear?

2. What needs to happen for sound to be produced?

Extensions

Exploring Pitch: Make Musical Glasses

1. Find six glasses that are exactly alike and fill them with different amounts of water.

2. Ask students to predict what will happen if they tap the glasses with a pencil. Will they make a sound? Will all of the glasses produce the same sound? Graph predictions and compare results.

3. Arrange glasses in order from the least water to the most and discuss the change in pitch from high to low.

Perceiving Sound: Game, In the Middle—Grades K–4

1. Blindfold one student and have him sit in the middle of the class.

2. Have the other students form a circle around him about 10 to 20 feet away.

3. Point to one of the students in the circle and have him say the seated student's name.

4. The seated person must then try to point in the direction of the voice and identify the name of the person who said his name.

5. Try this experiment with the seated student using both ears and then again with one ear covered.

Sorting and Classifying Data: Activity,
a Penny Saved Is a Penny Heard—Grades 3–6

Here is another way to test your hearing acuity:

1. Collect 10 or more U.S. pennies; the more you collect, the better the sample. The U.S. government changed the metals that it uses to make a penny. Pennies are not 100% copper anymore. For one thing, newer pennies look different. They also have a different sound.

2. Help students try to figure out when they changed the formula of the penny.

3. Explore the sounds produced by the pennies. Let students drop a collection of pennies, one at a time, on a hard surface like a table or floor. Newer pennies have a "tinny," "dull" sound. Older pennies have a more "full," "ringing" sound.

4. Use a magnifier and sort the pennies by year; order them from the oldest to the newest pennies.

5. Record the data and show the data on a bar graph. When did they make the switch to the new penny formula?

Some say that from 1983 on, pennies were made of copper-plated zinc. Do your data support this statement? Why or why not? (Lesson contributions from April Deese, 2002.)

GUIDED INQUIRY LESSONS USING A FIVE E'S FORMAT: INTERMEDIATE LEVEL—IT'S ALL IN THE FAMILY—A STUDY OF HEREDITY

Overview

This activity provides a simple example of the ways that genes are transferred from one generation to the next. Students will simulate gene transfer through two generations and discuss how the genes make family members similar to or different from one another.

Instructional Objectives

Following the activity, students will describe that traits are determined by hereditary information that is contained in genes, which are located in the chromosomes of cells. They will explain that individuals receive genetic information from their mothers and fathers, who got their genetic information from their parents. Further, they will demonstrate that sexually produced offspring are not identical to either of their parents.

Key Concepts From NSES

Heredity is the transmission of characteristics from parent to offspring by means of genes in the chromosomes.

Genes are the units of inheritance that pass from one generation to the next. Each gene carries a single unit of information.

Genes determine characteristics such as eye and hair color, blood type, and facial features, including dimples. An inherited trait can be determined by one or by many genes, and a single gene can influence more than one trait.

Human cells contain many thousands of different genes. Genes are responsible for the similarities in characteristics between parents and their natural born children.

Children resemble their parents and their grandparents because the genetic material in cells that is passed from one generation to the next carries information that determines traits. That information is carried on genes that are present in every cell of a person's body.

Resource

Genomics and Its Impact on Science and Society: The Human Genome Project and Beyond (2003) (http://www.ornl.gov/TechResources/ Human_Genome/publicat/primer/index.html)

Background Information

Genome

A genome is the complete set of instructions for making an organism. The genome is the master blueprint for all cellular structures and activities that occur during the lifetime of the cell or organism.

Found in the nucleus of every one of the many trillions of cells are chromosomes with tightly coiled threads of *deoxyribonucleic acid (DNA)* and associated protein molecules. If unwound and tied together, the strands of DNA would stretch more than five feet, but would be only fifty trillionths of an inch wide. The components of these slender threads encode all the information necessary for building and maintaining life for every organism from simple bacteria to complex human beings. Understanding how DNA performs this function requires some knowledge of its structure and organization.

DNA

A DNA molecule consists of two strands that wrap around each other to resemble a twisted ladder whose sides, made of sugar and phosphate molecules, are connected by rungs of nitrogen-containing chemicals called *bases*. Each strand is a linear arrangement of repeating similar units called *nucleotides,* which are each composed of one sugar, one phosphate, and a nitrogenous base. Four different bases are present in DNA: adenine (A), thymine (T), cytosine (C), and guanine (G). The particular order of the bases arranged along the sugar-phosphate backbone is called the *DNA sequence;* the sequence specifies the exact genetic instructions required to create a particular organism with its own unique traits.

The two DNA strands are held together by weak bonds between the bases on each strand, forming *base pairs* (bp). Genome size is usually stated as the total number of base pairs; the human genome contains roughly three billion base pairs. Each time a cell divides into two daughter cells (as in *mitosis*), its full genome is duplicated. For humans and other complex organisms, this duplication occurs in the nucleus. During cell division the DNA molecule unwinds and the weak bonds between the base pairs break, allowing the strands to separate. Each strand directs the synthesis of a complementary new strand, with free nucleotides matching up with their complementary bases on each of the separated strands.

Each daughter cell receives one old and one new DNA strand. The base pairing process ensures that the new strand is an exact copy of the old one. This minimizes the incidence of errors (mutations) which may greatly affect the resulting organism or its offspring.

Genes

Each DNA molecule contains many *genes*—the basic physical and functional units of heredity. A gene is a specific sequence of nucleotide bases, whose sequences carry the information required for constructing proteins, which provide the structural components of cells and tissues as well as enzymes for essential biochemical reactions. The human genome is estimated to comprise more than 30,000 genes.

Chromosomes

The three billion base pairs in the human genome are organized into 24 distinct, physically separate microscopic units called *chromosomes.* All genes are arranged linearly along the chromosomes. The nucleus of most human cells contains two sets of chromosomes, one set given by each parent. Each set has 23 single chromosomes—22 *autosomes* and an X or Y *sex chromosome.* (A female will normally have a pair of X chromosomes; a male will normally have a pair composed of one X and one Y chromosome.) Chromosomes contain roughly equal parts of protein and DNA; chromosomal DNA contains an average of 125 million base pairs. DNA molecules are among the largest molecules now known.

Chromosomes can be seen under a light microscope and, when stained with certain dyes, reveal a pattern of light and dark bands. Differences in size and banding pattern allow the 24 chromosomes to be distinguished from each other, an analysis called a *karyotype.* A few types of major chromosomal abnormalities can be detected by microscopic examination; Down's syndrome, in which an individual's cells contain a third copy of chromosome 21, is diagnosed by karyotype analysis. Subtle DNA abnormalities are responsible for many inherited diseases such as cystic fibrosis and sickle cell anemia, or they may predispose an individual to cancer, major psychiatric illnesses, and other complex diseases.

Materials

For each group of students: 24 colored candies, beads, paper shapes, marbles, plastic centicubes, or other small objects in the following colors: six red, six yellow, six blue, and six green; six small plastic, paper, or foam cups; pens or crayons—red, blue, yellow, and green.

Engagement

1. Ask students in what ways they are like their parents or grandparents. Are there traits that seem to run in the family, that is, that many family members have? Some inherited traits are: cleft chin, blue eyes, widow's peak, ability to roll your tongue, curly hair, attached ear lobes, and dimples.

2. What are some traits that you have that make you unique? Which of those traits make you most like your mother, father, or grandparents?

3. There are many ways that we are like our parents and grandparents. Why do you think there are similarities?

4. Ask students what they know about how features are transferred from generation to generation. Ask what they know about genes. Where have they heard about genes?

5. Determine what students know and don't know about genes and determine any misconceptions they have. Make a list of questions students have about genes and traits.

Prior Knowledge: Students should be familiar with the definition of genes so that the terms can be used in the activity.

Basic Definition: Genes are the structures that carry human traits from one generation to the next. Every cell in a person's body contains genes which are located on the chromosomes. Genes are the blueprints that determine what traits we have.

Scientific Definition: Genes are the basic physical and functional units of heredity. A gene is a specific sequence of nucleotide bases whose sequences carry the information required for constructing proteins, which provide the structural components of cells and tissues as well as enzymes for essential biochemical reactions. The human genome is estimated to comprise more than 30,000 genes.

Inquiry Question: How are genes, the carriers of human traits, transferred from one generation to another? Allow students to respond and share their ideas. Begin the investigation of their questions with this investigation.

Exploration

In this activity you will actually transfer "genes" from one generation to another to simulate the way that traits are transferred from one generation to another.

1. Place six small plastic cups on a table and label them as follows: *Grandmother 1, Grandfather 1, Grandmother 2, Grandfather 2, MOTHER,* and *FATHER.*

2. Place six red candies, plastic cubes, or other small objects in the Grandmother 1 cup and six blue objects in the Grandfather 1 cup.

3. Put six yellow objects in the Grandmother 2 cup and six green objects in the Grandfather 2 cup. The objects represent the genes that each grandparent has.

4. Without looking, select three objects from the cup marked Grandmother 1 and three objects from the cup marked Grandfather 1 and place them in the cup labeled MOTHER.

Table 3.1   Number of Genes for Each Child

Relative	Diana	Sam	Juanita	Charlie
Grandmother 1 (red)				
Grandfather 1 (blue)				
Grandmother 2 (yellow)				
Grandfather 2 (green)				
Total Genes				

5. Without looking, take three objects from the cup marked Grandmother 2 and three objects from the cup marked Grandfather 2 and place them in the cup labeled FATHER. We now have the genes for MOTHER and FATHER that were inherited from their parents.

6. Over the course of a few years, MOTHER and FATHER have four children–Diana, Sam, Juanita, and Charlie. These children will inherit traits from their parents.

7. Without looking, select three "genes" from the cup labeled MOTHER and three "genes" from the cup labeled FATHER and record their colors on the data table for Diana. Return the appropriate genes to each parent. Mix the genes in the cup.

8. Without looking select three genes from the cup labeled MOTHER and three genes from the cup labeled FATHER and record their colors in the space on the data table for Sam. Return the genes to their appropriate parent. Mix the genes.

9. Repeat the process for Juanita and Charlie. Record data on a table like the one shown in Table 3.1. Be sure to return the genes to each parent and mix them after recording the colors for each child.

Explanation

1. Why was it necessary to return the genes to the cup each time before selecting genes for another person? Discuss what is meant by "random sampling."

2. Suppose candy or plastic cubes were actually genes that determined some very obvious characteristics. Which of the children would be most alike? Which would be least alike? Explain.

3. Which child is most like Grandmother 1? Grandfather 1? Grandmother 2? Grandfather 2?

4. What do you think would happen if you had been working with hundreds of genes instead of only six?

5. What might happen if genes were damaged or destroyed before being passed along to a child? What is something that can damage or destroy genes?

6. What new inquiry questions do you have as a result of this investigation?

Elaboration and Extension

1. Trace a family history. Identify how traits such as hemophilia are carried or passed along from one generation to another.

2. Research some of the causes of mental and physical problems caused by damaged genes.

3. Research the human genome project.

4. Find out how mapping human genes will help us to deal more effectively with health issues.

5. Design a plan for investigating additional questions you have.

Evaluation

1. What do you know now that you didn't know before?

2. How has your learning changed your thinking about how traits are transferred from one generation to another?

3. What additional things would you like to know about heredity? Make a list of new questions you have. Design action plans for answering inquiry questions.

ANALYSIS

Analysis of *It's All in the Family* (Heredity):

Figure 3.2 shows some of the components of inquiry. Identify where each of the components of inquiry was addressed in the investigation.

Analysis of the Learning Cycle

Revisit the learning cycle model (see Figures 3.3-3.4). Identify the components of the Heredity activity that address each phase of the model.

Figure 3.2   Inquiry Links to *It's All in the Family*

Science as Inquiry	Links to *It's All in the Family*
Investigation	
Use of Logical Reasoning	
Data Collection & Analysis	
Use of Science Process Skills	
Manipulation of Materials	
Use of Evidence to Predict & Explain	
Recognize & Evaluate Alternative Explanations	
Think Critically & Logically	
Analyze Data	
Communicate Procedures, Results, & Explanations	
Formulate Questions Leading to Further Inquiry	

Figure 3.3   Connections Between the Learning Cycle and the Activity

Phase of Learning Cycle	How *It's All in the Family* Addressed Each Phase
Generate Questions and Problems	
Develop an Action Plan	
Investigate With Process Skills	
Collect and Process Data	
Form Conclusions; Process Thought	
Share Conclusions; Make Connections	
Ask New Questions	

Figure 3.4   Connections Between the Learning Cycle and Your Activity

Phase of Learning Cycle	How the Activity Addresses each Phase
Generate Questions and Problems	
Develop an Action Plan	
Investigate With Process Skills	
Collect and Process Data	
Form Conclusions; Process Thought	
Share Conclusions; Make Connections	
Ask New Questions	

CLASSROOM APPLICATION OF THE LEARNING CYCLE

Identify an area of your science curriculum and select an activity that is part of your curriculum or that you have done. Identify connections of the activity to the learning cycle.

Title of Activity:

Objective(s):

Key Concept(s):

Implications for the Classroom

Summarize how the use of the learning cycle model can help teachers address national and state learning standards and instructional goals.

Revisit the Initial Question

How does the use of a learning cycle model help to promote meaningful learning?

Essential #4: Inquiry-Based Science Builds a Greater Understanding of the Ways That Science, Technology, and Society (STS) Are Linked

4

In what ways does inquiry-based science build a greater understanding of the relationships between science, technology, and society? Review definitions of science, technology and society:

- *Science* provides explanations for observations about the natural world.
- *Technology* is the application of the principles of science; the many ways humans apply science to enrich and improve their lives.
- *Society* is the world in which the student lives as well as the expanded global community.

WHY STUDY THE RELATIONSHIPS BETWEEN SCIENCE, TECHNOLOGY, AND SOCIETY?

One of the primary goals of studying the relationships between science, technology, and society is the development of an informed citizenry capable of making wise decisions about both science and technology and acting on those decisions in a responsible manner.

The Education Committee of the Council of The City of New York (Committee on Education, 2004) points to another need for sound science education: to enable students to enter the rapidly expanding information technology and health care fields: *"Science training will be needed for 8 of the 10 occupational categories projected to have the fastest growth in the New York City region between 2000 and 2010: Computer Systems Administrators, Database Managers, Data Communications Analysts, Medical Assistants, Physical Therapist Aides, Occupational Therapist Aides, Physician Assistants, and Computer Software Engineers"* (p. 4; italics added).

We live in a technological world. Hand and machine tools operate throughout our homes, schools, offices and businesses, and industries to assist with solving problems, making work easier, and, generally, improving or enhancing the quality of life. The millions of technological innovations from can openers to solar-powered vehicles and from potato chips to computer chips have changed the way that we live, work, and play. And technology continues to advance at rapid rates.

The advancement of technology is dependent on creativity of thought and design; understanding of materials and resources; model building; functioning, durability, and practicality of products; and understanding of the trade-offs (environmental, economic, social, health, and emotional) associated with the implementation and use of the technology, among other things.

Environmental education has grown in interest and stature since Rachel Carson, a renowned author who wrote poetically about the complex web of life and the strength and resiliency of natural systems, pointed to the devastating effects of pesticides on the web of life in her controversial book, *Silent Spring*, first published in 1962 (2002). The book described in detail how DDT, the most powerful pesticide the world had ever known, entered the food chain and accumulated in tissues of animals, including humans, causing cancer and genetic defects. The book brought about public awareness of the vulnerability of nature and the consequences that technology had had and would continue to have on sensitive natural processes, if left unchecked. As a result of her efforts, DDT came under government supervision and was eventually banned. The Story of Silent Spring can be found at www.nrdc.org/health/pesticides/hcarson.asp

Fast forward to almost thirty years later when a single mother of three children, working at a law firm, discovered that a major power company knowingly used hexavalent chromium in its compressor plants—contaminating water and causing over 600 cases of serious illness, including cancer and miscarriages, in the community.

Technology, then, may be considered both a blessing and a curse. In many ways technology has enriched the lives of humans with few consequences to the environment. In other ways, technology is associated with enormous trade-offs and risks to health and the environment. It is important that students consider all sides—the benefits as well as the risks—of issues related to the use of technology for enhancing the quality of life and solving the problems of the world.

DEFINING THE RELATIONSHIPS BETWEEN SCIENCE, TECHNOLOGY, AND SOCIETY

When we hear the word *technology,* any one of a number of things may come to mind. Technology is evident in the many ways our lives are enriched. From a simple can opener to a complex nuclear power plant, technology provides humans with products and services that lie beyond their own capabilities.

Technology is often used synonymously with computers or other major types of equipment. Teachers often consider standards and goals that call for the use of technology in the classroom as a charge to include computer-assisted instruction and search for software programs that complement or supplement their instructional goals.

The goals of technology education extend beyond the use of computers and other large pieces of equipment. There are at least five different ways that technology can be perceived by educators and addressed through inquiry-based science. For all definitions of technology, it is important to recognize the links that exist between science and technology and to address the effects or impact on society—the lives of students, the local community, the state in which the student resides, the nation, and the global society.

TECHNOLOGY AS COMPUTERS AND OTHER AUDIOVISUAL EQUIPMENT

Throughout their school years, students become increasingly aware of the types and qualities of hardware available to them and the wealth of information available through audio, visual, and computer technology.

Radio, television, computers, and the Internet continue to offer a world of resources to teachers and students. Computer software, videotapes, CDs, and DVDs abound in the educational marketplace, bringing with them new learning tools such as probes and global positioning systems (GPS), information and research, virtual labs, microscopic and telescopic images, dissections, demonstrations, simulations, animations, online textbooks, and standards-based programs that enrich and enhance the learning process. This perception of technology is not to be discounted, as it continues to be a rapidly advancing medium for improving the quantity and quality of information that is available to the learner.

Thought and Discussion

1. Give examples of products that are used in your classroom or school that fit this category of technology.

2. How do computers and other hardware help students in your school or district to expand their learning opportunities and improve the quality of instruction?

3. Give examples of products that are used in the home that fit this category. What role do they play in the every lives of students?

TECHNOLOGY AS TOOLS FOR LEARNING

Instruments that apply the concepts and principles of science are a type of technology that enables scientists to learn more about the properties, quantities, distances and locations, and speeds of objects, as well as other natural phenomena. Technology provides the tools for investigative inquiry and analysis in the classroom. The products of technology enable students to extend their powers of observation and to engage in scientific investigation much like the scientist does.

In the primary grades, students use tools of technology to help them solve problems and learn more about the world around them. Simple pieces of equipment, such as magnifiers, thermometers, balances, rulers, measuring cups, and other such items, are used by students to extend their senses as they investigate their questions and solve problems.

Students use balances to compare the mass of objects and to investigate whether size or shape affect an object's mass or if two objects can have the same mass as one object. They practice the skills of measurement and apply the concepts of energy, gravity, force and motion, and speed by racing small cars down ramps of varying heights and comparing their results. The effects of gravity, lift, drag, and force can be realized when students design, create, and fly small kites.

As students move to the intermediate and middle grades, the tools and equipment become more sophisticated, and students soon realize that they can probe much deeper into the natural world through their use. Microscopes allow students to view structures that otherwise would not be visible. The better the microscope, the more magnification and clarity it provides. Sensitive balances provide the means for calculating mass and density with greater precision. Graduated cylinders, beakers, petri dishes, thermometers, probes, pulleys, wheels and axles, and other simple machines are just some of the materials that enable students to investigate as scientists, apply concepts and principles, and practice the skills of inquiry in the classroom.

Thought and Discussion

1. Give examples of tools and technologies that are available in your school or classroom.

2. How do these materials help students to expand their learning?

3. Give examples of tools and technologies that are used by students or their family members in their homes or in the community. How do students and their families use these materials to enrich their lives?

TECHNOLOGY AS CONCEPT APPLICATION

Challenges can be given to students that allow them to apply concepts. For example, students may learn that light usually travels in straight lines. Following an investigation of light rays, students may be challenged to design a system of three or more mirrors to reflect a light beam from the source—a flashlight—through the series of mirrors, to a spot on the wall—a target. The task requires students to work cooperatively to apply the law of reflection, demonstrating that the angle of incidence is equal to the angle of reflection. Then, students should find examples of this principle at school, at home, and in other familiar environments.

Following a study of the principles of aerodynamics, students may be challenged to design and test gliders, airplanes, or kites for their flying ability, thus experimenting with aspects of technological design and cause-and-effect relationships. Concepts related to flight, such as airflow and Bernoulli's principle, and to forces, such as wind, gravity, lift, and drag, can be studied in terms of how they affect patterns of flight.

Getting Started

Begin by finding books or programs that show examples of ways to apply the principles from the units of instruction you are teaching. For example, for principles of flight, such as gravity, thrust, lift, and drag, books such as *Flights of Imagination* (Hosking, 1990) and *The Sky's the Limit* (AIMS Education Foundation, 1987) provide an assortment of designs for kites, rockets, helicopters, airplanes, and gliders along with illustrations and instructions for constructing them using simple materials. In addition, these resources offer activities with clear procedures, data tables, and follow-up questions that can be embedded into the instructional program.

Science Olympiad is a competitive program through which teams of students are challenged to apply their knowledge and skills to tasks and problems. The Science Olympiad Web site, www.soinc.org, provides information and sample activities that address the application of science concepts and principles as well as technological design. State level Science Olympiad Web sites and competitions offer an array of challenges, including ideas for engaging students in experimental design such as building bridges and towers, testing architectural designs, identifying fossils, analyzing evidence for solving crimes, and testing understanding of topographic maps. Science Olympiad also relates to the dimension of Technological Design.

Thought and Discussion

1. Identify one or more key science concepts that you teach.

2. Identify applications of the concepts to everyday life, especially to the lives of children.

3. Discuss other ways you can apply the concepts and principles.

TECHNOLOGY AS PROBLEM SOLVING AND INVENTIONS

As students learn the basic concepts and principles of science, their applications of those concepts and principles bring about another dimension of technology and technological design: problems and inventions.

The solutions to problems that affect the society often involve technology. Solutions may take the form of changing policies and practices, or they may require the invention of new and better products to accomplish a task, or they may require building new structures, such as buildings, bridges, dams, tunnels, or domes.

Students may be curious about how products that they use every day, such as paper, plastics, synthetic fibers, metals and alloys, gasoline for buses and automobiles, glass, perfume, microchips, and the like, are manufactured.

They can be challenged to invent new ways to solve old problems (build a better mousetrap, invent a more efficient pencil sharpener, etc.) or to solve new problems through inventions or construction projects (more efficient routes or road construction, dams or power plants, more efficient energy production, etc.), recognizing that the designs of structures are important to their safe and effective functioning.

Technological solutions to problems often have trade-offs such as cost, safety, efficiency, or environmental quality. Sometimes the trade-offs are predictable and sometimes they are not. For example, the local community may have a large dam, a nuclear power plant, or other large power source that provides electricity. Through their research, students should become aware of the contributions that technology makes to the society and to their lives, as well as the trade-offs associated with them. Students will find that personal and social values often enter into decisions related to technology, prompting debate and discussion.

Begin dabbling in technological design with simple activities that align well with instructional goals. Resources similar to *Inventor's Workshop* (McCormack, 1981) provide a good introduction to using common materials in new and unusual ways or developing new and unusual ways to perform ordinary tasks. Directions are given for making purposeful contraptions such as water clocks, automatic candlesnuffers, and egg strength testers, along with inventive side trips composed of operational questions to expand the exploration of these products. Such resources filled with novel approaches provide teachers with tried-and-true samples that allow them to experiment with something new more confidently. Besides engaging students in the process of problem solving, selected tasks should relate directly to key concepts in science. Students should have to explain the concepts and the relationships between concepts that are learned through these unconventional approaches.

Students can trace the history of design changes in products such as automobiles, motorcycles, bicycles, and sports attire or sports equipment such as skis, ice skates, surfboards, or other items that interest them. For example, sporting goods companies use computational fluid dynamics software to simulate and test new models of swimsuits used by competitive athletes. Companies also map the human body by computer to aid in the design of suits for runners that provide added support, ventilation, freedom of movement, and muscle control.

Students should relate the structures of the products they research to their functions, be able to describe how the products changed over time, and describe how each of the new designs was innovative for the time period in which it was created. As a challenge, ask students to design a product for the future and describe how their new design will make the product better for a particular purpose.

Thought and Discussion

1. Identify one or more examples of technology used as problem solving or invention. How does the society benefit from the technology? What are the trade-offs associated with this technology?

2. Give examples of some inventions that have withstood the test of time and whose designs have changed throughout their history.

3. Relate the designs to the functions and describe how the change in structure affected function.

ENVIRONMENTAL PROBLEMS AND ISSUES

Social and environmental issues promote discussions of possible solutions, including technological solutions. Technology has provided lifesaving solutions to health problems, has led the way to the development of complex structures and sophisticated machinery, and has developed products and processes that rid the environment of harmful and hazardous wastes, but it is important to keep in mind that technology cannot solve all of society's problems. There are limits to technology and often the limits come in the form of increased costs, risks to health, safety, or efficiency, or destruction of the natural environment.

In every community, there are social or environmental problems or issues to investigate. For example, growing communities have to deal with the addition of power lines and increased demands for energy, water, and other natural resources. The loss of soil, vegetation, and green space; changes in the quality of air and water; added traffic and need for roads and other modes of transportation; destruction of animal habitats; loss of predators; decline of open space; and issues related to endangered species are just a few of the problems that accompany increased population and expansion.

Getting Started

Students should become aware of environmental problems and issues that affect their communities, their state, and their country. Analyses of problems and issues affecting the environment that are found in journals and newspapers on a daily basis can put students in touch with the ways that scientists approach, analyze, and solve or attempt to solve real-world problems. Inherent in these studies are the roles of science and technology and the affects and trade-offs to society and the environment. The development of community-wide, statewide, nationwide, and worldwide environmental ethics is critical to the survival of the planet.

One way to help students become aware of environmental issues is by having them review actual case studies and analyze such things as:

- the source of the problem or issue
- the observations that provide evidence of possible causes
- working hypotheses
- actions taken to deal with the problem or issue
- the reasons for the rules or policies governing the situation, if applicable
- possible solutions
- the current state of the art; next steps

Students may make recommendations for dealing with unsolved problems and issues. Two environmental issues related to animal extinction were (1) the dwindling habitat of the spotted owl in the Northwest due to timber harvesting, and (2) the loss and extraordinary recovery of the gray wolf population in Yellowstone National Park. With more than 1,200 species near extinction, there are plenty of case studies of this type to investigate.

By analyzing case studies, students can apply the vocabulary of science to real-world situations and develop a greater awareness of the ways that scientists think, operate, and solve problems. The example uses the vocabulary of science to analyze an environmental problem. Categories related to the problem-solving process may be selected to fit the details and contents of the article.

Analysis of a Case Study:
Large Numbers of Elk Die in Wyoming

The Associated Press reported a mysterious incident of elk die-off in southern Wyoming that brought about a thorough investigation of its cause ("Lichen Blamed for Mystery Elk Deaths," 2004).

Problem: Over 300 elk were found dead or dying in the Red Rim Wildlife Management Area of southern Wyoming in February of 2004.

Observations: Elk are very adaptable and able to survive on little food. Scientists tested animals for chronic wasting disease (elk version of mad cow disease); they ruled out most viruses and bacteria, malnutrition, exposure to toxic metals, poisoning from gas wells or pipeline leaks, and other possible causes.

Working Hypothesis: Researchers believed that the die-off was due to a chain reaction of several factors. More research was needed.

Next Steps and Strategies: Helicopters at the rate of $900/hour were used to search for afflicted elk; wildlife experts explored rough country to collect plant specimens and elk droppings. Further necropsy work was done to explore the physiology of the affected animals.

Findings: Parmelia molliuscula, a lichen that is found naturally in southwest Wyoming, was found in the stomachs of many of the affected elk. It contains an acid that apparently affected the muscle tissue of non-native elk that may have lacked the microorganisms necessary to neutralize the acid. When three elk at a research facility were fed a diet of the lichen, all three lost strength, were unable to function, and eventually had to be euthanized.

Theory: The *Parmelia molliuscula* lichen exists in an area where elk do not normally spend the winter. For some yet-unknown reason the elk moved into an area farther north than usual this year and many were unable to deal with the acid in the lichen. Some native elk were not affected, leaving researchers to believe that these animals had adaptations that enabled them to neutralize the acid in the lichen.

New Problems and Issues: Questions still remain about whether elk have eaten *Parmelia molliuscula* in other years, and, if so, why the die-off hasn't occurred before. The area has had a history of drought—what affect might that have had on the situation? What implications are there for management and improvement of the range lands? Approximately five percent of the females were affected by the die-off. How might this affect hunting quotas in the future or change wildlife policies? What other steps may need to be taken to prevent future die-offs?

Thought and Discussion

1. Discuss the environmental problem in terms of science, technology, and society. In what ways was technology involved in the study? In what ways is the society affected by the situation? What are the trade-offs related to the solutions (cost, risks, and/or benefits)?

2. Give an example of an environmental problem or issue in your community or state that directly or indirectly affects the lives of students. What about this issue might be of interest to students? What are some questions students might ask?

3. Suggest some ways students might investigate the problem or issue.

TECHNOLOGY AS A PRODUCTION SYSTEM

Technology can involve many individual components—machinery and processes—working together to produce products or provide services to humans. Complex assembly lines for manufacturing products, ranging from automobiles to candy bars and cheesecakes, are made up of an array of machinery, often interspersed with human interactions, with each piece designed to accomplish a specific task. Systems may focus on a marvel of technology, such as a high-speed railway system or airport system, and include the related physical and human components that allow such systems to function efficiently and effectively for the benefit of the society.

Getting Started

Concepts and principles related to mechanical energy are explored in the AIMS activity book, *Machine Shop* (AIMS Education Foundation, 1993). This excellent resource provides hands-on instructional activities that allow students to investigate and learn the principles of mechanical energy by studying simple machines.

Visit a large transportation system—airport, train station, or bus terminal. Apply the principles of energy to the system. Identify the roles of technology and society (humans) within the system. What are the benefits of these systems to society? What are the risks, costs, and trade-offs?

Visit a manufacturing plant, research the assembly-line process involved in manufacturing products that are familiar to students, or invite a representative of a manufacturing plant to visit the school. Design a set of interview questions to ask during a visit. Questions related to structure and function of equipment, use of energy, system performance and maintenance, cost factors, quality control, environmental concerns, and efficiency of operation might be asked. Students should become aware of the role of technology and the role of human workers in the system. Identify the careers that are associated with the operation of the production system.

APPLYING TECHNOLOGICAL DESIGN IN THE CLASSROOM

Technological design includes studies in a number of related fields. Some of these fields are engineering, architecture, and industrial design. To meet the standards related to technological design, students should engage in problem solving by designing, building, and testing solutions to real-world problems. Through the problem-solving tasks, students will apply critical thinking skills and content knowledge, and compare and assess technological devices for such things as cost, benefits, applications, practicality, environmental impact, safety, and convenience.

The goals and objectives for technological design call for students to develop skills to:

- identify and state a problem, need, or product
- apply critical, coherent, and independent thought to the design and development of a product or a solution to a problem
- design solutions to problems and analyze the effectiveness of designs
- analyze cost, risks, and benefits of solutions or products
- implement and evaluate the solution or product
- accurately record and communicate observations and findings

Although some of the goals can be reached through cognition, activities that require students to make drawings or illustrations of ideas or products or to actually produce and test the ideas or products are far more powerful learning approaches. An important consideration throughout instruction should be the development of basic knowledge and skills of design as used in art, engineering, architecture, and industrial design curricula.

Students can become aware of technological design through resources such as *The Way Things Work* (Macaulay, 1988) that not only describe machines, physical science concepts, and the history of many inventions in words, but provide detailed drawings and illustrations that show their intricate workings. Spatial perception can be enhanced through resources such as *Incredible Cross Sections* (Beisty, 1992) where students are introduced to the seldom seen, intricate components of trains, huge buildings, castles, boats and submarines, a space shuttle, and more.

Global and national ecological and health-related problems and issues are often reported in the media. Students become aware of state and local issues at school and through local newspapers, radio, and television, and through their involvement in clubs, organizations, special interest groups, or recreational activities. They are often curious about environmental and health issues, such as pollution (air, water, and land), energy sources, and alternative forms of energy; problems related to animals, such as animal rights, animal abuse, and extinction; and diseases and afflictions that affect people, such as heart disease, AIDS, cancer, and others that may have affected family members and friends. Automobile safety is also an area of interest as the highways become more crowded and dangerous for young motorists.

Most of these problems and issues have direct connections to technology and to technological design. As students become aware of how these problems and issues are being addressed, they gather information, consider possible solutions, identify and discuss trade-offs, and develop action plans for reasonable solutions that may be supported by plans, blueprints, model structures, new products, and other technologies that they create. Exploring the ways that problems and issues play out in the social world enables students to see their relevance in their own lives. Through their study, students will become familiar with professional careers in science and technology along with the roles and contributions of the professionals in the society.

The Lifelong Kindergarten research group directed by Mitchel Resnick at the Massachusetts Institute of Technology is developing new technologies that enable students to learn in new ways. Their rationale is described in Dr. Resnick's essay, "Playful Learning and Creative Societies" (2003) and can be found at http://www.educationupdate.com/archives/2003/feb03/issue/child_playfullrng.html

The MIT Lifelong Kindergarten projects include Learning Through Designing, Technological Fluency, and Bridging the Digital Divide. These and other projects are described on the Web site: http://web.media.mit.edu/~mres/

ACTIVITIES THAT ENGAGE STUDENTS IN PROBLEM SOLVING AND TECHNOLOGICAL DESIGN

The samples given here are not new, but they provide examples of ways that simple problem-solving tasks can be linked to scientific thought, key concepts of science, history of science, and technological design. It is important to engage students without losing sight of what is most important: the learning. Students need to plan, organize, and reflect on the experiences so that they understand why they are doing the activity and to link the tasks and results to key concepts, problem-solving processes, applications of concepts, design, and other instructional goals.

Sample Challenge #1: Egg Drop

A good example of a challenge that engages students in problem solving and technological design, yet does not require a lot of time or materials, is a simple egg drop. There are many ways that this activity may be structured.

Procedures: Begin by asking students what would happen if you were to drop a raw egg to the ground from a height of three meters. Most students will be aware of the fragile nature of eggs and the force that attracts objects to the center of the earth: gravity. The following activity challenges students to design a container to lessen the force of gravity.

Materials: Per team of students: 15 straws; 10 craft sticks; one meter of masking tape (other materials may be used, such as small foam cartons that provide a uniform size for egg containers, and scrap materials).

Challenge: In this task, students are asked to design a container that will prevent an egg from breaking when it is dropped from a height of approximately three meters.

Part of the egg must be visible after it is secured in the container.

Thinking: Students will be using logic, reasoning, and creative thought as they design and make their containers. Students can compare designs that worked with those that did not.

Key Concept: Gravity is the force that makes objects fall to the ground. It is also the force that keeps organisms and objects on the ground and the planets in their orbits around the sun.

Related Activities: Many elementary activities require students to overcome the force of gravity in order to accomplish a task, such as flying a kite. Students will experience the effect of gravity on objects that fall. Students may also study the ways gravity affects the orbits of planets and comets in the solar system and how it affects the rise and fall of tides.

History of Science: Research how gravity was discovered and learn more about the work and theories of Isaac Newton (1642–1725), Johannes Kepler (1571–1630), and Nicolaus Copernicus (1473–1543) related to gravity.

Engineering: Engineers study ways to overcome gravity when they design rockets and airplanes. They also investigate how gravity affects objects pulled downward in a straight path, such as elevators, and objects pulled downward on curved paths, such as roller coasters.

Sample Challenge #2: Investigating Force

In this task, students are challenged to design and build a structure or group of structures that will exert an upward force on a mass that is equal to the opposite downward force exerted on the mass by the earth.

Materials: Per group of students: 20 pieces of uncooked spaghetti or other shapes, such as linguini or fettuccini; and one meter of masking tape. Safety goggles for testing designs; books, bricks, or other heavy objects for testing the strength of the structures—in order to compare structures, all groups should use the same or similar objects.

Challenge: Build a structure using 20 pieces of pasta and one meter of masking tape that will support the greatest mass. The completed structure must support the mass at least five centimeters above the table. Experiment with a variety of designs for the structures.

Testing Strength: When testing strength of structures, be sure to wear safety goggles. Begin by placing one object (book, brick, or other heavy object) on the completed structure; add additional objects of the same type to determine the total number of objects the structure can support. What will happen when the downward gravitational force on an object exceeds the upward force exerted by the structure on which it rests? Determine where the strongest and weakest parts of the structure are.

Key Concept: An object is supported by a structure when the downward force of gravity acting on the object is balanced by the upward force exerted by the structure. When the gravitational force on an object exceeds the upward force on the object exerted by the structure on which the object rests, the structure will break. When opposing forces are balanced, there is no net force acting on the object, and the *F* in the equation *F = mass times acceleration* is zero. Both sides of the equation must be the same and, since the mass is not zero, the acceleration must be zero. Thus, when the forces are equal and opposite there is no change in motion.

The object falls when the downward force is greater than the upward force exerted by the structure. The excess downward force breaks the structure, and the object accelerates toward the center of the earth until it strikes some other force. When the object is at rest, the opposing forces on it are equal.

Thinking: Students will use creative problem-solving skills, logic, and reasoning as they design, build, and test the structures.

(Lesson modified from Gartrell, 1989, pp. 82–84.)

Sample Challenge #3: Paper Bridges

A simple sheet of paper is used in this activity to hold up a mass of 100 pennies or other small objects of similar mass. Concepts of compression and tension are investigated as students design and test paper bridges.

Materials: Per group of students: one sheet of plain paper; five paper clips; ruler; two books or blocks of equal size; 100 pennies or small objects of similar mass; scissors.

Challenge: Build a bridge that spans 20 centimeters between two books or blocks and can support the mass of 100 pennies. Discuss ways to make paper strong enough to support a mass as well as itself.

Place the books 20 centimeters apart and make the bridge high enough for a boat to pass below it. Test each bridge design by putting one penny or object on it at a time. Record the number of pennies or objects per design. Modify the design to hold more mass. Compare the bridge's ability to support the weight in one spot versus the weight spread out.

Design Rule: The sides of the bridge should rest on the two books and cannot be taped or attached to the books or to the table.

Key Concepts: A bridge must support its own weight as well as the weight of anything placed on it. Adding mass to the bridge causes stress; the top portion compresses, while on the bottom portion tension is created. Tension is a stress that tends to pull an object apart. Changing the shape of something can change the way it resists forces. Paper can be folded, rolled, or twisted to support weight.

Science and Engineering: Scientists and engineers use models to test their ideas before they apply them to building large structures.

Thinking: Students will use creative problem-solving skills, logic, and reasoning as they design, make, and test their bridges.

(Lesson modified from Building Big Educator's Guide, http://www.pbs.org/ wgbh/buildingbig/educator/act_ paper_ho.html)

Other challenges using simple materials are:

- Build the tallest tower you can using only two sheets of newspaper. Modify the design using 20 centimeters of tape or modify so that the tower can support a golf ball, an eraser, a candy bar, or another small object.
- Build the tallest free-standing structure using 15 straws and 10 small pieces of masking tape. The structure must remain standing upright for 10 seconds. Add a challenge: Build the tower so that it can support a golf ball (or other small object).

Studying large construction projects is another way of learning or applying concepts. Compression and tension are two key concepts that can be explored through the designing and constructing of model bridges and buildings and testing their strength. David Macaulay offers a wealth of information on the construction of bridges, domes, skyscrapers, and tunnels in *Building Big* (Macaulay, 2000). The book is a companion to a television series of the same name (Klein, 2000) that describes historical, social, and environmental problems and issues associated with the building of large structures and identifies planning and design problems that eventually had to be solved.

Technological design allows students to develop a greater appreciation for the work of scientists and engineers. Through the design process students develop or reinforce their understanding of concepts and principles of science and develop problem-solving skills while using their imagination and creativity. Such challenges not only engage students in student-centered, thought-provoking tasks that target multiple learning goals, but they allow for a variety of ways for students to use a variety of multiple intelligences.

USING TECHNOLOGICAL DESIGN TO SHOW CONCEPT UNDERSTANDING: UNDERSTANDING ADAPTATION

Biological evolution accounts for the diversity of species developed through gradual processes over many generations. Species acquire many of their unique characteristics through biological adaptation, which involves the selection of naturally occurring variations in populations. Biological adaptations include changes in structures, behaviors, or physiology that enhance survival and reproductive success in a particular environment.

Grades 5–8: Create a Creature

Standards: Diversity and Adaptation of Organisms

In Part I of this activity, students will investigate properties and characteristics of the planets in the solar system (other than Earth) and add their data to a table showing:

- number of hours in a day (maximum and minimum)
- surface temperature—day and night
- gravity compared to that on Earth
- gases
- clouds
- period of orbit around the sun
- other features about which students have questions

In Part II of the activity, students will apply the concept of adaptation to the design of a creature that can survive in the conditions of a selected planet. Students will select a planet and, using the information in the table, design a creature that can live comfortably on that planet. Students will share their creatures and explain the features (adaptations) that allow it to survive in the conditions on the planet. Note a possible misconception:

Students may believe that adaptation means that individuals change in major ways in response to the environmental conditions, just as they would not be able to immediately adapt to an environment without oxygen. Adaptation takes a great deal of time and change.

Background Information

After researching the characteristics of the planets, students may want to know something about the features found on planets before designing their creatures. Students should research the features about which they know little or have questions, as this information may inform their designs. Some of the features described in the planet information are:

Greenhouse Effect: "The greenhouse effect is the rise in temperature that the Earth experiences because certain gases in the atmosphere (water vapor, carbon dioxide, nitrous oxide, and methane, for example) trap energy from the sun. Without these gases, heat would escape back into space and Earth's average temperature would be about 60° colder. Because of how they warm our world, these gases are referred to as greenhouse gases" ("Greenhouse Effect," n.d.).

Hydrogen: Hydrogen is colorless, highly flammable gaseous element, the lightest of all gases, and the most abundant element in the universe. Symbol is *H*; atomic number 1.

Helium: Helium is a light inert gas and the second most abundant element in the universe. Helium, *He*, was discovered in 1868 by J. Norman Lockyear in the spectrum of a solar eclipse.

Sodium: Sodium is a chemical element in the periodic table that has the symbol *Na* and atomic number 11. Sodium is a soft, waxy, silvery reactive metal belonging to the alkali metals; it is abundant in natural compounds (especially salt water and halite). It is highly reactive, burns with a yellow flame, oxidizes in air, and reacts violently with water, forcing it to be kept under oil.

Carbon Dioxide: Carbon dioxide is a heavy colorless gas (CO_2) that does not support combustion, dissolves in water to form carbonic acid, is formed especially in animal respiration and in the decay or combustion of animal and vegetable matter, is absorbed from the air by plants in photosynthesis, and is used in the carbonation of beverages. CO_2 is one of the greenhouse gas chemical compounds.

Nitrogen: Nitrogen was discovered by the Scottish physician Daniel Rutherford in 1772. It is the fifth most abundant element in the universe and makes up about 78% of the earth's atmosphere, which contains an estimated 4,000 trillion tons of the gas. The symbol for nitrogen is *N*.

Argon: Argon was discovered by Sir William Ramsay, a Scottish chemist, and Lord Rayleigh, an English chemist, in 1894. Argon makes up 0.93% of the earth's atmosphere, making it the third most abundant gas. Argon is obtained from the air as a byproduct of the production of oxygen and nitrogen. The symbol for argon is *Ar*.

Methane: Methane is a colorless, odorless, flammable hydrocarbon (CH_4) that is a product of decomposition of organic matter and of the carbonization of coal. Methane is one of the greenhouse gas chemical compounds.

Ammonia: Ammonia (NH_3) has a penetrating odor. It is the active product of smelling salts, a compound that can quickly revive some one who has fainted. Ammonia is a toxic, reactive, and corrosive gas that can make one very ill. It can, in fact, be fatal. Ammonia is pretty nasty stuff. Nevertheless, it is also an extremely important bulk chemical widely used in fertilizers, plastics, and explosives.

Water: Water is a clear, colorless, odorless, and tasteless liquid with the symbol H_2O. It is essential for most plant and animal life, and is the most widely used of all solvents. Water has a freezing point of 0 degrees Celsius (32 degrees Fahrenheit) and a boiling point of 100 degrees Celsius (212 degrees Fahrenheit).

Sulfuric Acid: Sulfuric acid is a highly corrosive, dense, oily liquid, colorless to dark brown depending on its purity. Symbol is H_2SO_4. It is used to manufacture such things as fertilizers, paints, detergents, and explosives.

Instructional Goals

After researching the conditions that exist on the planets, students will be able to compare conditions on the earth with those found on other planets.

Students will show an understanding of adaptation through the design of a creature and be able to explain the ways that the features of the creature allow it to survive on a planet.

Students will communicate verbally their understandings of the concept of adaptation.

Materials

References and resources for researching conditions and features of the planets.

Engagement

So far, scientists have not discovered any aliens living on other planets. Suppose a being were found to live on another planet? What would it be like? How would it be similar to or different from humans on Earth?

What would you need to know about the planets to answer the above questions? NASA scientists have asked you to help them to identify the types of features that might be found in aliens living on other planets. They would like to keep a file of possible aliens and features that allow these aliens to survive on the planets. They have asked you to create a creature that might survive on one of the other planets.

Exploration

Part I

In this activity, students will be researching conditions and features of the planets. They should make a list of research questions related to planetary features. A chart should be designed so that students can record information.

Note to Teachers: Figure 4.1 shows information that was collected by students for each of the planets: the number of hours in a day (maximum and minimum), the number of hours in a night (maximum and minimum), the surface temperature day and night, gravity compared to the gravity on Earth, gases on the planet, cloud cover, and other features. Charts will vary with student interests and questions.

The design and development of the chart might be a group project where two or three students (singly or as a group) might research a single planet and share information with others to create the chart. As students research features, new questions may arise about atmospheric components and geographic features. Allow students to research their questions.

Part II

Individually or with a partner, students should create a creature that can survive on a planet other than Earth. When creating this creature, they must consider at least five of the characteristics of the planet listed on the Planet Information Sheet.

Figure 4.1   Planet Information Sheet

Planet	Density g/cm³: Earth = 5.52g/cm³	Surface Temp (max/min or mean) degrees K	Gravity: Earth = 1	Atmospheric Components	Cloud Cover	Length of Year (Earth Days)	Length of Day (Earth Days)	Other Features
Mercury	5.43	700/100	0.39	trace amts of H & He	none	88 days	58.65 days	Craters, valleys, mountains; (Caloris Basin is 1,350 km dia)
Venus	5.25	Mean surface temp: 726; Temps can be 800° F+	0.91	96% CO_2; 3% N; 0.1% water vapor; thick – pressure = 90X Earth	Thick clouds of CO_2 & sulfuric acid	224.7 days	243.02 days (back-wards)	Volcanoes, craters, mountains; greenhouse effect; basaltic rock
Mars	3.95	310/150 (temps plunge to negative 200° F)	0.38	95% CO_2; 3% N; 1.6% Ar (only planet with atmosphere & temp. similar to Earth)	Very thin water & CO2; only planet to have an atmosphere similar to Earth	687 days	1.026 days	Volcanoes & valleys; mountains, polar ice cap; iron oxide dust; basaltic rock; high point Olympus Mons is 24 km above plains
Jupiter	1.33	Mean surface temp 120	2.6	90% H; 10% He; .07% CH_4	Very thick CH_4; NH_3	4,329 days or 11.86 years	0.41 days or 9.8 hours	Great Red Spot; infrared spectra imply dark rock fragments; giant storm; faint ring
Saturn	0.69	Mean surface temp 88	1.07	97% H; 3% He; .05% CH_4	Very thick CH_4; NH_3	10,753 days or 29.46 years	0.44 days or 10.2 hours	Rings = 270,000 km in dia.; ice particles or covered w/ ice; traces of silicate use silica & C minerals; liquid & metallic H & He; spins fast; stormy; lightning; liquid surface
Uranus	1.29	Mean surface temp 59 (−345° F)	0.9	83% H; 15% He; 2% NH_3	Thick	30,685 days or 84 years	0.72 days or 17.9 hours (back-wards)	System of narrow, faint rings; dark particles; rocky or carbonaceous material
Neptune	1.64	Mean surface temp 48	1.15	74% H; 25% He; 1% CH_4; (deep, w/ 1,200 mph winds)	Thick	60,190 days or 164.8 years	0.67 days or 19.1 hours	Giant storm area = Great Dark Spot; ocean of H_2O, NH_3, & CH_4; faint rings

(Continued)

Figure 4.1 (Continued)

Planet	Density g/cm³: Earth = 5.52g/ cm³	Surface Temp (max/ min or mean) degree s K	Gravity: Earth = 1	Atmospheric Components	Cloud Cover	Length of Year (Earth Days)	Length of Day (Earth Days)	Other Features
Pluto	2.03	Mean surface temp 37	0.05	CH_4; N2	Not found	90,520 days or 248 years	6.39 days (back- wards)	Perhaps methane ice
Earth	5.52	310/260	1	78% N; 21% O_2; 1% Ar	Varied	365.26 days	23.93 hrs. = 1 day	Highest point Mt. Everest 8 km + above sea level; basaltic and granite rock

Reference: $°K = °C + 273$ $°F = 1.8° C + 32$

Student Assignment: Draw the creature on large poster paper or newsprint and give it a name. Write a story or clear description of the alien, including its adaptations and the advantage of each adaptation for survival.

Presentation: Be ready to show your creature and describe how each characteristic is adapted to the conditions on the planet by providing an advantage for each adaptation that helps the creature survive.

For Example: Camels have adapted to life in the desert by having long eyelashes (adaptation) to keep sand out of their eyes (advantage) and wide hooves (adaptation) for walking in deep sand (advantage).

Explanation

Questions to Discuss

1. What planet did you select? Why did you select that planet?

2. Describe your creature and tell what adaptations it has for life on the planet.

3. What adaptations are similar to those of humans? What adaptations are different from those of humans? Explain what you learned about adaptations.

4. What new questions do you have about the conditions on your planet and the ability of your creature to survive in those conditions?

Evaluation

1. Analyze the creatures. Determine if the adaptations of the creatures and the reasons for the adaptations fit the conditions that exist on the planet.

2. Determine if students have accurately described adaptations and the reasons for them.

3. What evidence shows that students understand the concept of adaptation as it applies to life on Earth and other planets?

BUILDING TECHNOLOGY AND TECHNOLOGICAL DESIGN INTO THE CURRICULUM

Technological design can be used as part of an activity where concepts that are learned through investigation or research are applied to the creation of a product. For example, following a study of simple machines:

• Students might create a Rube Goldberg–type of system using a variety of simple machines to accomplish a specific task, and describe the role of each machine in accomplishing the task. For resources, see rubegoldberg.com

• Students might design a brochure that shows a detailed drawing of an invention from the past (at least 50 years old) that is made up of a number of simple machines (printing press, paper bag, water wheel, "hobby horse," 1904 automobile, calculator, typewriter, etc.). They could identify and label the simple machines that make up the compound machine, tell why the machine was invented, describe what the invention looks like today, draw a picture of the inventor and give some biographical information, and identify the resources used.

Or following an activity where students discover the unique properties of colloids, students might design uses for the unusual material they investigated or design a spacecraft that can visit and successfully leave a planet made of the unusual material, thus demonstrating their understanding of the properties of the substance. (Lesson idea from GEMS Module–Oobleck, Lawrence Hall of Science, Berkeley, CA.)

Research questions and projects that require students to apply the concepts they are learning should be added to units of instruction to enhance meaning, including those that address the nature of science, such as historical events and the people who have made contributions to scientific knowledge throughout history, the work of current scientists, and the nature of scientific projects funded by national and private foundations.

Example: Unit—Earth in Space

Sample Questions Related to Science and Technology

1. How much and what types of information about galaxies do astronomers have? What are the shapes and sizes of three types of galaxies? What instruments are used to view these or provide information about them?

2. Research the theories of the origin of the universe.

3. Study photographs from the Hubble Telescope and discover how these photos enhance our understanding of the universe. See photos at www.jp.nasa.gov

4. Design a brochure describing a trip to outer space. Design the spacecraft that will transport the passengers and create a travel guide for the trip. Include the equipment, resources, and safety devices that would be needed for the journey, such as heat shields, space suits, food, sources of oxygen, etcetera.

5. Telescopes: Trace the development of telescopes from the early telescopes of the 1600s to the Hubble of the 1990s. How did the technological advancements and discoveries over time change our perception of the universe? Make a graphic organizer to show a sequence of important events in the history of the telescope. Design a telescope for the future that will be able to go "beyond Hubble." The Web site http://hou.lbl.gov/ will be helpful.

6. NASA employs people from many different academic fields such as astronomy, earth systems science, planetary science, space physics, chemistry, mathematics, computer science, graphics and technical writing, accounting, and business management. Learn more about these and other professional careers related to space science. Find out what kinds of questions scientists are attempting to answer. What will be the questions of the future? Helpful resources include:

   http://nssdc.gsfc.nasa.gov

   http://spacelink.nasa.gov

Example: Unit—Populations and Ecosystems

Sample Questions Related to Science and Technology

1. What are the most common plants and animals that live in your area? What factors of your environment allow for these plants and animals to exist there? What plants and animals would you like to know more about?

2. Are there any species of plants or animals in your area that are nearing extinction? Find out what can be done to protect them.

3. It is predicted that the tropical rainforest has many species of organisms that have not yet been discovered. These plants and animals may provide valuable contributions to the field of medicine. Learn more about the importance of the tropical rainforest and the organisms that thrive there.

4. The rainforest is slowly disappearing from the earth. Find out how you can help to save it. Design a plan for saving the rainforest! For resources, see www.ran.org/info_center/

5. What was the role of fire in the maintenance of the prairies of the Great Plains before agriculture? Why did naturalists recently say that the fires in Yellowstone National Park were long overdue? Research the role of fire in the maintenance of natural environments. Design a maintenance plan for the National Park System.

6. Agricultural practices such as crop rotation, use of recommended planting rates and row widths, the improvement of plant varieties, fungicidal sprays, and the efficient use of irrigation systems have been used to control erosion and diseases. Compare management strategies that do not use technology with those that use technology. Learn more about these and other practices. Which of these (or other) practices are used in your geographic area? Are there ways these practices affect you personally?

Students can identify environmental problems or issues that are of interest to them and design inquiry questions to investigate. For each inquiry question, they should identify the problem, design an action plan, research information, identify possible solutions, weigh alternatives and trade-offs, and make recommendations for solving the problem. They should identify and share lists of human and other resources for learning about problems or issues.

Other Resources

1. The American Society for Engineering Education provides information and resources that promote engineering education in Grades K–12. See www.engineeringk12.org

2. The Society of Automotive Engineers is an organization of engineers, business professionals, educators, and students from over 97 countries who share information and exchange ideas for advancing

the engineering of mobility systems. They offer hands-on physical science curriculum materials for Grades 4-10. See www.sae.org

3. Down the Drain is a collaborative online classroom project designed by the Center for Improved Engineering and Science Education (CIESE). Recommended for Grades 4-8, this exercise allows students to collect data from around the world to see how other areas' water usage compares to ours at home. See www.k12science .org/curriculum/drainproj

Revisit the Initial Question

In what ways does inquiry-based science build a greater understanding of the relationships between science, technology, and society?

Essential #5: Inquiry-Based Science Provides Experiences Necessary to Support and Develop or Modify Interpretations of the World

5

How does inquiry-based science influence the ways students interpret the world? Students come to school with preconceived notions about the natural world based on their backgrounds, prior knowledge, and experiences. Their theories tend to be based on how the world appears to operate and their attitudes and values related to learning are formed through the experiences they have had. Books, TV, video games, and movies may portray the natural world in unscientific ways. Experiences without mediation to guide learning or discrepant events that make science seem magical may lead to a confusion of ideas or misconceptions.

MISCONCEPTIONS

Are you aware of any misconceptions students have based on their worldly experiences, TV programs, lack of formal education, or discrepant events in their lives? Discuss.

The videotape *Private Universe* (Harvard-Smithsonian Center for Astrophysics, 1987) shows that even well-educated individuals develop and cling to misconceptions about the natural world. The program provides valuable insights into the ways misconceptions are developed.

Analyzing Misconceptions: Case Study

Problem: Following an instructional unit on water and the water cycle, students were asked to explain why water droplets form on the outside of a cold glass on a warm day. One student explained the phenomenon by writing that the water inside the glass seeped through the glass to form drops on the outside of the glass.

1. Describe the student's misconception.

2. What would be a possible reason for her explanation?

3. What is the key concept that she does not understand?

4. What might be done in the instructional unit to correct this misconception?

5. How will the teacher know when the misconception is corrected?

Key Concept: There is water vapor in the air, and the amount depends on such things as the availability of water and the temperature of the air. Warmer air contains more water vapor than cooler air. When warm air comes in contact with a cold object, such as a glass containing a cold liquid, the air surrounding the glass is cooled and the water vapor from that air condenses to form droplets on the glass.

USING DISCREPANT EVENTS IN THE CLASSROOM

The Upside: The use of discrepant events in the classroom can be an exciting way to capture student attention and promote interest, questions, and discussion. As students observe the event, they are often captivated by what they see and hear going on. They are left puzzled but amazed and, often, curious!

Discrepant events make great introductory activities for instructional units and set the stage for instructional activities that will resolve the mystery behind the discrepant event and take students to the next level of concept understanding.

The Downside: Discrepant events may appear to be magical rather than scientific to the learner if something happens that does not have an immediate, recognizable cause and effect. To many students, watching the discrepant event is like watching a magic trick. Without mediation, guided learning, and resources and references, students may make interpretations of the events that have little to do with science. When they cannot understand what caused the event, students may make up a reason that is less than scientific, developing a misconception, or reinforcing their beliefs that science is weird or that science is only for smart people, increasing a fear or mistrust of science.

The Solution: Simply providing an explanation for a discrepant event is generally insufficient, since it does not enable the learner to act on or develop an understanding of the concepts and principles underlying the event. A simple explanation is not a substitute for developing a mental model or thinking frame for a concept. Mediation is the key to the successful use of discrepant events. Discrepant events should be used wisely and in conjunction with a set of learning activities that allow the learner to grasp the *why* of what happened in the discrepant event. As with all learning, teachers must monitor the path to concept development carefully, selecting instructional strategies and experiences wisely and using frequent formative assessments to monitor student thinking.

Example: Discovering Bernoulli's Principle

Give each student a strip of paper and have students make a fold about three centimeters from one end.

Hold the paper strip at the folded end and blow *under it*. Observe what happens.

Now, ask students what they think will happen when they blow *over* the strip of paper.

Hold the fold of the paper at your bottom lip and gently blow outward over the paper strip. Observe.

Most students will experience something other than what they predicted if the prediction was based on prior knowledge of gravity, force, and motion. If left without mediation, these students are likely to be confused. Through questioning, teachers can lead students to the understanding of a new concept. From there, students can apply the principle in a new context. Questions should focus on the observations and experiences students had, with links to additional knowledge that will help them construct the new concept.

Questions for Discussion: Unraveling the Mystery

1. What did you observe when you blew under the paper?

2. What did you observe when you blew over the paper?

3. What do we know about the properties of stationary air?

4. What is different about the air on top of the paper compared to the air under the paper when we blow over it?

It is obvious that to understand the discrepant event, something must be known about air pressure and the relationship between air pressure and speed of movement. If students are not led to an understanding of air pressure in a way that explains the event, they will never be able to comprehend the event and realize that the reason for the mysterious behavior was, in fact, scientific.

Explanation: Stationary air exerts pressure in all directions. The air that blew over the paper strip was moving faster than the air that was under the paper strip. The pressure in a fluid (air) decreases as the speed of the fluid increases. Therefore, the air with the higher pressure below the strip was exerting greater pressure on the paper than the air above was exerting. The paper was pushed into the lower pressure region.

Principles

1. Force is the push or pull on an object. With stationary air, there is an even force on all sides of the paper.

2. Gravity is a force that causes objects to fall downward. Without an additional force, the paper falls downward due to gravity.

3. The pressure in a fluid decreases as the speed of the fluid increases. Therefore, the air above the paper strip was exerting less pressure than the air below the strip.

4. Daniel Bernoulli, a Swiss scientist of the 18th century, studied the relationship between fluid speed (in this case, air is a fluid) and pressure. His discovery is called Bernoulli's principle.

   Bernoulli's principle is represented by the formula $P=KE/V$, where P = pressure; KE = Kinetic Energy; and V = volume

(Lesson modified from Demonstration 2.1 in T.L. Liem's *Invitations to Science Inquiry*.)

Have students repeat the event with new information and then apply the principle in new contexts until they are able to develop an experience base for Bernoulli's principle.

MEDIATED LEARNING EXPERIENCES

Mediation implies that teachers are consciously aware of what they do and how they do it in order to structure the best possible conditions for learning. Using frequent and relevant feedback from students, they guide the learning process. Often this practice is underrated, thought to occur naturally, or taken for granted. Effective mediation of classroom instruction encompasses important aspects of instructional planning and delivery, cognitive intervention, best practices, and use of strategies.

A useful operational definition is offered by Dr. Meir Ben-Hur in his article "Mediation of Cognitive Competencies for Students in Need" (1998).

Mediated learning experiences transform our cognitive systems and facilitate our cognitive development. Mediators confront us with and draw attention to selected stimuli.
   In doing so, they:

      Schedule the appearance and disappearance of stimuli

      Bring together stimuli that are separated by time and/or space

      Focus attention on transformations in stimuli that we otherwise might overlook

Dr. Ben-Hur further defines the characteristics of mediated learning experiences:

Intentionality: The teacher interposes him/herself intentionally and systematically between the children and the content of their experiences.

Reciprocity: Both teachers and students reciprocate with shared intentions. Teachers use questions and/or varied experiences to create student-felt needs for mediation.

Transcendence: Mediated learning experience seeks changes in the way students learn and think. Changes must transcend, that is, go beyond the content and context.

Meaning: Meaningful learning may be considered the successful product of emotional and cognitive excitement.

The use of questioning throughout the learning process promotes the development of meaning, since questions help to keep students focused on the concepts and skills to be learned and provide immediate feedback to teachers about what students are learning. Key questions should be built into the instructional plan.

Thought and Discussion

1. What must a student know in order to grasp the science in discrepant events?

2. How do instructional activities help students develop a greater understand of the key concepts?

3. How do misconceptions distort student interpretations of the world?

4. What are some ways teachers can add components of mediated learning to their instruction?

DISPOSITIONS

Another important consideration on the road to scientific literacy is the development of dispositions that are valued by the scientific community. Working scientists exhibit behaviors that have become a part of their nature and define the work they do. These qualities and characteristics constitute the dispositions that underlie science. Teachers who exhibit enthusiasm for science and model the dispositions provide a powerful influence on the attitudes toward science that are developed by students. It is only when students are given opportunities to engage in the process of inquiry (act as scientists) that are they able to practice and instill the dispositions of science.

Dispositions That Underlie Science

- *Curiosity and a Desire for Knowledge:* Scientists have an innate or developed desire for knowing and understanding the world.

- *Cooperation:* Scientists share ideas, theories, and techniques at the local, state, national, and international levels.
- *Having Confidence In and Relying on Data:* Scientists respect evidence, which also implies the testing and retesting of ideas and monitoring of one's own thinking processes.
- *Comfort With Ambiguity:* The results of science are always tentative; testing and retesting provide more confidence in one's conclusions; ambiguity gives rise to new problems and questions.
- *Respect for Living Things:* All living things deserve human care, both in the lab and in the field. Our attitudes toward the care and handling of live organisms say much about our value systems as human beings.
- *Willingness to Modify Explanations:* Additional data or reinterpretations of existing data may require us to modify explanations for phenomena and events; willingness to rethink conclusions is often one of science's and science learning's most difficult personal decisions.
- *Respecting and Trusting the Thinking Process:* Science is an active process defined by patterns of reasoning that lead to theory building and theory testing; trust in the process is an essential element.

Thought and Discussion

1. Discuss ways that teachers can model each of the dispositions of science.

2. Adopt one or more of these new ideas and apply it to your classroom instruction.

3. How will the modeling of dispositions by teachers and the applications of these to experiences in the classroom help students interpret and/or modify interpretations of the world?

4. Identify professional development initiatives that would help teachers to better understand and model the dispositions of science.

Revisit the Initial Question

How does inquiry-based science influence the ways students interpret the world?

Summarize main ideas from Essentials 1–4. How do the types and number of concepts and skills students learn; the connections of concepts students make to their lives, to technology, and to society; and the dispositions they observe and model shape, support, or modify their interpretations of the world?

Essential #6: Inquiry-Based Science Enhances Reading and Writing Skills

6

What are some of the ways that inquiry-based science enhances reading and writing skills? The ability to integrate prior knowledge with new information is a key factor in building concepts and deeper meaning. For learning to take place, new words and concepts need to be explained or learned in ways that link them to familiar words and prior knowledge. Science-related reference books, software programs, posters, charts, and other electronic and printed resources are useful for enhancing the understanding of new terms and concepts. Often the new vocabulary and explanations given in reference materials are accompanied by colorful drawings, precise illustrations, clever animations, or actual photographs that capture interest and define meaning. It is important that students hear and use new vocabulary in classroom dialog and discussion and use the vocabulary in writing assignments, lab reports, and journal or notebook entries.

ANALYZING CURRENT EVENTS THROUGH ARTICLES

Active reading strategies such as identifying main ideas, selecting supportive data and relevant information, making inferences, elaborating, and giving explanations can be applied to technical reading and research reports as well as to journal articles and news accounts. For example, when students find articles that describe a scientific event or discovery, an environmental problem, or other significant information, they can summarize the important components by identifying such things as:

- the source of the information
- the main idea: problem or discovery
- observations and methods
- working hypothesis or inquiry question
- strategies used in investigation or in problem solving
- findings
- theories resulting from the problem-solving process or discovery
- new questions, problems, investigations, issues, etcetera.

These are just some suggested headings under which information can be outlined. There may be others that are more appropriate to the articles. Teachers may have to assist with suggested headings at first, but, eventually, students should decide the headings to be used for summarizing their findings.

An analysis of an article from the NASA Web site might look like this:

What Neil and Buzz Left on the Moon

http://science.nasa.gov/headlines/y2004/21jul_llr.htm

Source: In July, 2004, a news release from NASA identified the most important thing that Neil Armstrong left on the moon.

Main Idea: Neil Armstrong left a boot-shaped depression in the Sea of Tranquility on the moon 35 years ago, but he also left a two-foot-wide panel with 100 mirrors pointing to Earth. The device is a "lunar laser ranging retroflector array." Astronauts Buzz Aldrin and Neil Armstrong put it on the moon on July 21, 1969. It is the only Apollo science experiment still in operation.

Inquiry Questions: The mirrors are used to "ping" the moon with laser pulses and measure the earth-moon distance. Inquiry questions are related to the moon's orbit and to theories of gravity.

Strategies: A laser pulse shoots from a telescope on Earth, crosses the earth-moon divide, and hits the array. The mirrors send the pulse straight back to where it came from. The round trip travel time pinpoints the moon's distance with precision.

Observation Site: A key site is the McDonald Observatory in Texas.

Findings: The moon is spiraling away from the earth at a rate of 3.8 centimeters per year.

Theories: The earth's ocean tides are responsible. The moon probably has a liquid core. The universal force of gravity is stable.

Findings: Newton's gravitational constant (G) has changed less than one part per billion since the experiment began.

Other Questions: Scientists used the laser to check Einstein's theory of gravity, the general theory of relativity. Einstein's equations predicted the shape of the moon's orbit as well as laser-ranging can measure it.

New Questions: Some physicists believe that the general theory of relativity is flawed.

New Inquiry: NASA and the National Science Foundation are funding a facility in New Mexico, the Apache Point Observatory Lunar Laser-ranging Operation (APOLLO). Researchers will examine the moon's orbit to get measurements precise to within one millimeter, which is ten times more precise than measurements currently being made.

Guided reading activities require students to access and use information and put them in touch with the latest scientific research, current problems and issues, and recent discoveries in science. They are able to view science as an ongoing process, to "meet" some of the key researchers, and to realize that science is a human endeavor that has both successes and failures. Students realize that scientific investigations take time and that theories are constantly modified or changed as more data are collected, sometimes through the use of more sophisticated technology.

Using References and Resources: Students can reinforce their learning when, following observations and investigations, they have access to reference and nonfiction books such as the Eyewitness Books (Alfred A. Knopf, New York) and the Reading Expeditions series from the National Geographic Society (www.ngschoolpub.org/). Such resources provide a wealth of information and visual stimulation to the learner. The colorful images illuminate the pages while student-friendly text, using the vocabulary of science, defines terms and explains concepts. Materials such as these provide depth of content, reinforce key concepts, and add another dimension to the learning experience.

INTEGRATING WRITING

One of the main goals of a science program is for children to understand and apply science concepts. Writing in science is a powerful tool that improves vocabulary, sentence structure, and organizational skills. Because students have to process information prior to writing, students develop an understanding of science concepts to a greater degree when they write about them.

Some ways that writing can be incorporated into the science lessons:

- In a notebook, have students write a prediction, describe a set of procedures and a conclusion for an activity or experiment, and write a follow-up summary or article reporting the results.
- Data tables or charts can have space for students to write descriptions or explanations.
- If students receive a letter from a prominent person (a principal, a community leader, a celebrity, etc.) asking them to investigate something, they can follow up with a letter describing what was done and the results of their study.
- Students might write letters to prominent people or organizations, such as the head of the school board or an elected official, the Chamber of Commerce, the Environmental Protection Agency, or the Alzheimer's Association, requesting information and asking questions.
- Have students write a story related to the theme of the unit—for example, after studying erosion, students could write a story about the journey of a rock from one location to another, describing what happens along the way. Primary grade students might write a sentence or two describing how the shell they are studying got onto the beach. Following the study of the water cycle, students could be asked to write a first-person account of a falling drop of water; or following a study of fossils, students could make a drawing of the reconstructed animal or plant and write a story about its prehistoric life.
- Notebook entries should be rich with descriptions of investigations, predictions, data tables and charts, data and conclusions, discussion questions and answers, and key concepts and vocabulary. In addition, statements of learning and applications of learning (drawings, illustrations, diagrams, graphic organizers, research questions, research data, problems and issues, etc.), should be notebook entries.

USING SCIENCE NOTEBOOKS

Using notebooks for science investigations causes students to focus attention on the content and on the process of science. Many science programs include the use of notebooks or journals that are used by students to record observations, describe action plans, collect data, summarize findings, and create written and visual explanations to show understanding of science concepts. Notebooks may also include summaries of articles, Web searches, research, essays, and stories that complement the classroom work.

Notebook entries provide a basis for answering questions related to what was done; they should include observations and inferences, data that were collected and recorded, and conclusions that were drawn. Students will be more likely to engage in group discussions based on what they did and what they learned if they have the support of their notebooks. Sharing data may identify discrepancies, leading to further investigation and new questions.

Inquiry-centered science programs that emphasize the use of student notebooks have been found to increase the language proficiency test scores as well as the science achievement test scores of participating students. Scores on state-mandated science achievement tests also showed significant gains for students participating in inquiry science programs that used notebooks (Lapp, 2001).

DESIGNING SCIENCE NOTEBOOKS

The use of science notebooks is an excellent way to integrate writing into the science curriculum. A science notebook might include any or all of the following components:

Inquiry Questions or Problems of Interest

- essential question or problem in student's own words
- why question or problem is important and how it relates to instructional goals, big ideas, or key concept(s)

Prediction

- shows connections to prior experience or knowledge; may identify misconceptions
- is clear and reasonable; relates to question; shows thought

Note: It is important for students to realize that a prediction describes knowledge or perceptions prior to an investigation. The prediction may be based on limited or no prior knowledge, and it is not expected that the prediction will be correct. Therefore, it is not necessary for a student to change a prediction once the data are collected. There should be no penalty for an incorrect prediction. What is most important is this: If the prediction is not correct, the student recognizes that the original thought or perception was not accurate and understands how the evidence or data gathered in the investigation support the change in knowledge or perception.

Action Plan for Investigating Inquiry Questions

- The plan is reasonable and relates to the inquiry question.
- The plan shows a clear sequence of events and directions.
- The variable that will be investigated is identified (and others, if appropriate).
- The plan includes a data table; materials are listed.

Observations and Data

- Observations and data relate to the inquiry question and action plan.
- Multiple types of data are included: drawings, charts, graphs, numbers, writing, etcetera.
- Observations and data are well organized and accurate for the investigation.

Conclusions and Summaries of Learning

- Students identify the "aha" or observations and insights learned through investigation.
- Clear statements of learning and key concepts are included; may include reflective thought.
- Statements are based on inquiry question and procedures, and are supported by data or evidence.
- Student makes connections to technology and society, where applicable.

Next Steps/Formulating New Questions

- Students identify new questions and related interests.
- Questions are extensions or applications of original inquiry question.
- Questions are worthy of investigation or research.

Teacher and Student Reflection

- Student identifies science content, process skills, and dispositions embedded in activities.
- Student links science to math, language arts, social studies, and other areas of the curriculum; student describes the importance of integrated (contextual) learning.
- Student recognizes and values learning that captures the essence of the disciplines.

Thought and Discussion

1. Analyze the use of the notebooks. Discuss how the notebook entries capture evidence of concept development, process and thinking skills, and dispositions.

2. Design a science notebook page to use with any one of the activities that are presented in this book or an activity that you use in your classroom.

USING A SCIENCE NOTEBOOK TO ENHANCE READING, WRITING, MATH, AND THINKING

Comparing the Strengths of Magnets

Design a notebook to be used with this intermediate grade activity.

This activity may be part of a unit on magnetism and electricity or on force and motion; it is presented as an inquiry that requires students to design their own investigations. Prior experience of students should include the study of ways to design tests to make comparisons between variables and to test the effects of one variable on another.

Students should have been taught to:

- generate a formal question that describes what they are testing
- write a hypothesis
- think through and describe procedures they would use to test the question
- identify what variables will be held constant in the experiment and what variable will be tested
- design data tables; conduct tests; record data; construct graphs
- draw conclusions based on data

Variation: The activity may be used to introduce students to the above processes. The teacher will need to make changes in the structure of the activity in order to guide the students through the stages of the investigation. In either case, the notebook will be a valuable component for recording the process of inquiry and the learning that occurs.

Materials: two different types of magnets; paper clips or other magnetic objects; balances and mass sets; graph paper; paper and pencils

Inquiry Question: How Do the Strengths of Two Different Magnets Compare?

To engage students, they may be given a role to assume where their research findings are important to a cause. Or, they may be asked to investigate this phenomenon for other reasons that are of interest to them. In any case, they should make careful entries in their notebooks for every phase of their work.

Procedures

1. Design a test to compare the strengths of two different magnets.

2. Write the research question and a hypothesis.

3. Write a description of the procedures, including the variable that was tested and the variables that were controlled. Include multiple trials for greater accuracy.

4. Conduct the test and collect and record data in a data table.

5. Graph the data and label all parts of the graph.

6. Write a short summary of the conclusions in the form of a report. Include the research question, a hypothesis, procedures used for the test, variables tested and controlled, data table and data, a graph of the data, and a conclusion.

Thought and Discussion

1. Share your notebook with others.

2. Use the following criteria to score your notebook.

Criteria for Scoring Notebooks

Notebooks will vary depending on the design of the investigation. However, the following components should be included in the notebook:

1. an appropriate hypothesis

2. identification of variables that were controlled

3. identification of the manipulated (independent) variable

4. clear procedures: a clear description of the steps used

5. data table with appropriate and reasonable responses; evidence of multiple trials

6. a logical and accurate conclusion supported by data

7. a bar graph with appropriate title, labels, and data

8. a written report of summary of conclusions as stated in #6 above

In addition, indicators of science inquiry should be evident; the work should show that the student:

9. conducted a scientific investigation

10. used appropriate tools and techniques to gather, analyze, and interpret data

11. used logic and reasoning to show the relationships between evidence and explanations

Developing Thinking Skills Through Analysis and Creative Writing

Literature also provides a context for addressing new concepts and vocabulary. Well-crafted stories and poems that relate to scientific information may offer content in new and novel ways. Students can analyze passages for meaning and identify the science through questions and discussion. Composing or analyzing prose or poetry related to science content activates creative as well as critical thinking skills. Instructional objectives in language arts may also be addressed in this way.

For example, the following poem can be analyzed during a study of human body systems.

Ballad of a Boneless Chicken

I'm a basic boneless chicken,
Yes, I have not bones inside,
I'm without a trace of rib cage,
Yet I hold myself with pride,

Other hens appear offended
By my total lack of bones,
They discuss me impolitely
In derogatory tones.

I'm absolutely boneless,
I am boneless through and through,
I have neither neck nor thighbones,
And my back is boneless too,

And I haven't got a wishbone,
Not a bone within my breast,
So I rarely care to travel
From the comfort of my nest.

I have feathers fine and fluffy,
I have lovely little wings,
But I lack the superstructure
To support these splendid things.

Since a chicken finds it tricky
To parade on boneless legs,
I stick closely to the hen house,
Laying little scrambled eggs.

Thought and Discussion

1. *Reading strategies:* Identify the main idea in the poem. Identify some cause-and-effect relationships. Find the meaning of words such as *derogatory, splendid,* and others that might be unfamiliar to students. Distinguish between fact and fiction. What is the author's purpose and message? Predict how the chicken would be different if she had a skeletal structure.

2. Make a Venn diagram to show similarities and differences between life as a boneless chicken and life as a chicken with bones.

3. *Links to science:* The poem relates well to the study of the skeletal system. Develop a set of questions that can be used to analyze the poem and focus on the function and importance of the skeletal system. Develop one or more inquiry questions related to the skeletal system.

4. Draw the boneless chicken and explain ways that it is similar to and different from a chicken with bones.

5. *Creative writing:* Use the example as a model and ask students to write a (short) creative poem that relates to another body system. The poem should relate to the both the structure and the function of the system.

ANALOGIES

Developing analogical thought is an important instructional goal that can be developed through the K-8 science experience. As part of the processing of inquiry experiences, questions dealing with similarities and differences in structures, cause-and-effect relationships, structures and function in living and nonliving things, relationships of persons to places, and such build a base for understanding analogies.

Douglas Hofstadter offers a useful definition of analogical thought and an explanation of the two components of analogies:

Analogical thought is dependent on high-level perception in a very direct way. When people make analogies, they perceive some aspects of the structures of two situations—the *essences* of those situations, in some sense—as identical. These structures, of course, are a product of the process of high-level perception.

It is useful to divide analogical thought into two basic components. First there is the process of *situation-perception,* which involves taking the data involved with a given situation, and filtering and organizing them in various ways to provide an appropriate representation for a given context. Second, there is the process of *mapping.* This involves taking the representations of two situations and finding appropriate correspondences between components of one representation with components of the other to produce the match-up that we call analogy.

Hofstadter, Douglas, and the Fluid Analogies Research Group,
Fluid Concepts and Creative Analogies: Computer Models
of the Fundamental Mechanisms of Thought.
(New York: Basic Books, 1995)

Analogies in Science

Some of the types of relationships that might be considered in the context of science are shown in Figure 6.1.

Figure 6.1   Types of Analogies and Examples

Type	Analogy
Part to Whole	Wing: Bird :: Arm: Human
Cause & Effect	Spicy Food: Indigestion :: Dust: Sneeze
Time	Prophase: Mitosis :: Starting Line: Race
Gender	Stallion: Mare :: Boy: Girl
Antonyms	Hot: Cold :: Left: Right
Group and Member	Bird: Duck :: Reptile: Turtle
Symbol	Smokey the Bear: Fire Safety :: Red Light: Stop
Creation/Creator	Painting: Artist :: Vaccine: Scientist
Age	Kitten: Cat :: Tadpole: Frog
Function to Object	See: Eye :: Hear: Ear
Person to Place	Curator: Museum :: Scientist: Laboratory
Object to Tool	Planet: Telescope :: Slide: Microscope
Synonyms	Taste: Observe :: Write: Record

Thought and Discussion

1. Create an analogy that relates to one of the units or topics in your curriculum.

2. Identify the category.

3. Identify the analogical thought process: situation/perception and the mapping for the analogy.

4. Share your analogy.

Revisit the Initial Question

What are some of the ways that inquiry-based science enhances reading and writing skills?

Essential #7: Inquiry-Based Science Allows for a Diversity of Strategies for Learning

7

How does inquiry-based science allow for the use of methods and strategies that promote student learning? Classrooms abound in diversity. In multicultural environments, diversity exists in many ways, including in the ways students learn. Inquiry-based science is a natural approach for providing a variety of choices for how students will learn the concepts and the relationships between concepts they are investigating.

Drawing on learning styles research (Gregory & Chapman, 2002; Samples, Hammond, & McCarthy, 1985; Silver, Strong, & Perini, 2000), as well as on Gardner's (1993, 1999) theory of multiple intelligences, theories of emotional intelligence (Golman, 1995), the theory of "flow," (Csikszentmihalyi, 1990, 1993), and other theories, and recognizing the cultural diversity in the classroom, teachers are encouraged to be creative in providing a variety of ways and a variety of contexts to enhance student learning.

ANALYZING LEARNING

Pretest

1. Describe the way(s) you learn best.

2. Identify one learning experience from science that was very meaningful for you as a student, that is, in which you really learned something.

3. Give an example of a classroom activity you might use as a teacher that is similar to the meaningful experience that you had.

In the late 1970s Howard Gardner began a study dealing with the nature and realization of human potential that culminated in his 1983 publication in which he synthesized his research and posed a theory of multiple intelligences. The theory expands well beyond the notion of differing talents and focuses on a number of separate human capabilities that are fundamental to the individual. "An intelligence entails the ability to solve problems or fashion products that are of consequence in a particular cultural setting or community." Gardner further describes the importance of these: problem-solving skill allows one to approach a situation in which a goal is to be obtained and to locate the appropriate route to that goal. Creation of a cultural product, such as a scientific theory or a musical composition, is critical to capturing and transmitting knowledge or expressing one's views or feelings (Gardner, 1993, pp. 9 and 15).

Dr. Gardner's eight intelligences are described briefly in Figure 7.1.

Figure 7.1   Gardner's Eight Intelligences

Intelligence	Exhibited by
Linguistic	Gift of language; ability exhibited in its fullest form by poets and writers
Logical-Mathematical	Logical, verbal, and mathematical ability; includes "scientific thinking" (computer scientist)
Spatial	Ability to form a mental model of a spatial world; to maneuver and operate using a model (engineers, surgeons, painters, sculptors, navigators)
Musical	Ability to think, create, and perform musically
Bodily-Kinesthetic	Ability to solve problems or fashion products using one's body (dancers, athletes, surgeons)
Interpersonal	Ability to understand people, what motivates them, how they work, how to work with them; sensitivity (salespeople, teachers, clinicians, religious leaders)
Intrapersonal	Capacity to form an accurate, truthful model of oneself and to use that model to operate effectively; access to one's own life/feelings/emotions
Naturalistic	Expertise in recognition and species classification; sensitive to and comfortable with nature; perceptual skills (gardeners, animal trainers, naturalists)

Implications for Education

Gardner supports a "less is more" principle and the notion of defining *endstates* based on a set of important concepts and performances as the basis of curriculum and assessment. Further, he contends that ideal assessment should search for genuine problem-solving or product fashioning skills in individuals.

Gardner's principle may be applied in a classroom environment at the K-8 level as students demonstrate their understanding of concepts and principles of science and of the process of inquiry to solve problems and answer questions they have about the natural and social worlds. In addition, the creation of products that reflect conceptual understanding and process and thinking skills provide further evidence of student learning.

Thought and Discussion

1. How does having an understanding of multiple intelligences theory (and others related to teaching and learning) help teachers design and plan for meeting the diverse needs and interests of students in the classroom?

2. Identify some of the ways that multiple intelligences can be addressed in instruction or assessment in the science classroom. Compare your list to the ideas of others and to those that are suggested in the list of strategies in Figure 7.2.

METHODS, STRATEGIES, AND BEST PRACTICES

The concepts and principles of science and the skills of inquiry are the end products of science education. The development of these along with the skills of thinking and problem solving through high quality classroom instruction should begin early in a child's education.

The terms *methods, strategies,* and *best practices* are commonly used in educational settings. They are not mutually exclusive categories, as there are obvious overlaps. The distinction that will be made between these three categories is one that is based on operation:

Figure 7.2 Strategies for Instruction or Assessment Linked to Multiple Intelligences

Strategies for Instruction or Assessment Linked to Multiple Intelligences	
Linguistic	Reading and vocabulary development Formal speech, debate, discussing ideas and plans with peers Journal or notebook keeping Poetry or creative writing; humor and storytelling Sharing information from reading and research
Mathematical	Use of abstract symbols and numbers, graphing data Use of graphic organizers to show understanding Calculation and problem solving Use of estimation, application, and reasoning
Spatial	Guided imagery and imagination Color schemes, patterns, designs, and drawings Using scale, making models
Musical	Finding patterns Music and rap: composition and performance related to concepts Exploring sounds in the environment
Bodily-Kinesthetic	Role playing, drama, and mime Physical gestures to show movement of animals Human graphs and models Inventing Applications of concepts using physical activity Demonstrating concept understanding through movement
Interpersonal	Giving feedback, describing findings, elaborating on concepts Cooperative learning strategies and collaborative skills, group projects Showing empathy and concern for practices that adversely affect animals, humans, and the environment Sensing motives
Intrapersonal	Reflecting and focusing on one's own thinking Designing action plans based on reasoning Working individually, engaging in personal research and study
Naturalistic	Exploring, discovering, and investigating Organizing and patterning thought Asking questions and probing the natural world Making observations using the senses; classifying information and creating classification systems Using the outdoors as a learning environment and to demonstrate understanding

- *Methods* are the traditional ways that science education has defined the various approaches to teaching.
- *Strategies* are the creative inclusions that enhance the methods and allow teachers to increase motivation, create greater interest through variety, challenge students, address multiple intelligences, create opportunities for collaboration, vary perspective, etcetera. Strategies require creative input and often add novelty to a lesson.
- *Best practices* are lists of classroom teaching behaviors that link to increased student achievement. These practices are generally research based and may include methods and strategies.

Methods

Methods are few; they are powerful approaches to learning. They are linked to belief systems and expectations of administrators, parents, and students; they are the choices that are made about how students will be engaged in learning; often, they are teacher dependent. All of the methods have merit; each method is useful for specific purposes. High quality instruction includes the use of a variety of methods.

Methods of science teaching are described in Figure 7.3, along with emphases from the National Science Education Standards, which are reflected in many state and district curriculum guides. Thought and consideration should be given to methods as they relate to content standards.

Thought and Discussion

1. How would you describe the relationships between the NSES content standards and the instructional methods?

2. Discuss how a variety of methods can be used to achieve the goals of the NSES and state or district curriculum guides.

3. What are the implications of this relationship for curriculum design and delivery?

Strategies

Strategies are many and varied; they are the creative ways that methods are enhanced and used to their greatest extent to increase student learning. They are tools, organizational structures, activities, or approaches that are added to a basic instructional plan that make learning fun, challenging, manageable, interactive, child-centered, thoughtful, and interesting.

Marzano, Pickering, and Pollock (2001) offer a research-based set of categories of instructional strategies that have links to student achievement. The categories of strategies are:

1. identifying similarities and differences

2. summarizing and note-taking

3. reinforcing effort and providing recognition

4. homework and practice

5. nonlinguistic representations

6. cooperative learning

7. setting objectives and providing feedback

8. generating and testing hypotheses

9. questions, cues, and advance organizers

Figure 7.3   Methods for Teaching Science Linked to NSES Content Standards

Emphasis in Content Standards (NSES)	Basic METHODS for Teaching Science
Understanding scientific concepts and developing abilities of inquiry	**EXPOSITORY** Read, watch videos, listen to lectures or a speaker, receive information
Learning subject matter disciplines in the context of inquiry, technology, science in personal and social perspectives, and history and nature of science	**DEMONSTRATION** Generally passive observation of a product or process, may include student interaction or discussion
Integrating all aspects of science content	**DISCUSSION** Teacher- or student-initiated conversation; involves some or all students; requires prior knowledge, reading, research, or activity
Studying a few fundamental science concepts	**GUIDED INQUIRY/DISCOVERY** Hands-on investigations with focused inquiry; lab activities often with predetermined results but may include investigations with varied results; may be projects or products; may be based on student questions or interests and include activities, experiences, and research; teacher is mediator and guides instructional activities
Implementing inquiry as instructional strategies, abilities, and ideas to be learned	**OPEN INQUIRY** Problem-based, student constructed inquiry; generally based on student questions or on predetermined problems; approach has little structure; teacher's role is facilitator; teacher may design context, but students determine what to do and how to do it; results are not predetermined; alternative solutions are offered and considered

Figure 7.4 Instructional Strategies

Think, pair, share	*Humor in the classroom*	*Use of music, songs, raps*
Positive affirmation	K-W-L charts; generating questions	Debate
Movement	Firsthand experiences	Cooperative grouping and teaming
Graphic organizers or mind maps	Field trips	Jigsaw
Peer review and self-assessment	Identifying similarities and differences	Reflective thought
Instructional games	Creating models	Videotape, film, broadcast
Using the Internet	Use of outdoors; field trips	Interviews
Roundtable discussion	Role playing	Data analysis
Use of essential questions	Analyzing a story, dilemma, or issue	Guest speaker
Using notebooks	Presentations	Gallery walk
Research projects	Designing posters, brochures, newsletters, or fliers	Science centers

Detailing the strategies that can be used in the effective classroom is beyond the scope of this book. However, the list in Figure 7.4 will serve to identify some of the many strategies that are found in the literature and are available to classroom teachers to use to create a classroom where students have the greatest opportunity to learn.

The Creative Use of Strategies

1. Select one (or more) strategy that you know well and use often. Share details and examples of the strategy.

2. Discuss ways the strategies that are well known and commonly used apply to one or more of the six categories of instruction:

   • motivation
   • creating or maintaining a context
   • process of instruction—activities, student input, modeling, investigation, discovery
   • processing information

- checking for understanding
- extending learning

3. Select one (or more) strategy that you do not know well or commonly use. Learn how the strategy might be used to enhance instruction and promote learning in the science classroom. Apply new strategies to classroom instruction.

Best Practices

Best practices are teaching behaviors steeped in philosophy, since how we perform as teachers in the classroom is based, to a large extent, on our beliefs about the teaching and learning process.

Best practices, too, are linked to student achievement. The Best Practices From NSES Teaching Standards offer a vision of teachers and students working together as active learners. (see Figure 7.5 on page 119). Effective classrooms emphasize inquiry approaches that engage students, develop student responsibility for learning, incorporate formative assessment, encourage cooperative and collaborative approaches, and focus on understanding.

Thought and Discussion

Compare best practices to methods and strategies:

1. In what ways are best practices *similar to* methods and strategies?

2. In what ways are best practices *different from* methods and strategies?

3. Identify the strategies that can be used to differentiate instruction and provide for the needs of a diversity of learners.

4. Identify ways that methods, strategies, and best practices are used in the sample activities throughout this book.

Revisit the Initial Question

How does inquiry-based science allow for the use of methods and strategies that promote student learning?

Figure 7.5   Best Practices From NSES Teaching Standards

Less Emphasis On	More Emphasis On
Treating all students alike and responding to the group as a whole	Understanding and responding to individual student's interests, strengths, experiences, and needs
Rigidly following curriculum	Selecting and adapting curriculum
Focusing on student acquisition of information	Focusing on student understanding and use of scientific knowledge, ideas, and inquiry processes
Presenting scientific knowledge through lecture, text, and demonstration	Guiding students in active and extended scientific inquiry
Asking for recitation of acquired knowledge	Providing opportunities for scientific discussion and debate among students
Testing students for factual information at the end of the unit or chapter	Continuously assessing for understanding
Maintaining responsibility and authority	Sharing responsibility for learning with students
Supporting competition	Supporting a classroom community with cooperation, shared responsibility, and respect
Working alone	Working with other teachers to enhance the science program

SOURCE: Reprinted with permission from National Academy of Sciences, *National Science Education Standards* (Washington, DC: National Academies Press, 1996).

Essential #8: Inquiry-Based Science Allows for a Variety of Ways for Students to Show What They Know and Are Able to Do

8

FUNDAMENTALS OF ASSESSMENT

In what ways does inquiry-based science allow students to show what they know and are able to do? An assortment of tools can be used to gather evidence of student learning of concepts, skills, and dispositions of science. The *Assessment Tool Kit* defines a variety of ways that evidence of student learning can be captured and recorded. The information can then be used to modify, guide, and assess the instructional process. The Assessment Tool Kit includes:

- *Observation Checklists:* Use of checklists or other written documentation to record behaviors that show skill acquisition, valued dispositions, and other evidence of student achievement.

- *Interviews and Dialogue:* Teacher-to-student or student-to-student oral questioning and discussion to clarify understanding of concepts and skills, to identify problems or issues, or to determine attitudes and values.

- *Learning Logs, Notebooks, and Journals:* Use of student-developed text, action plans, questions, written documentation of process, data, graphs, inferences, conclusions, new questions, etcetera. Purposeful entries are those that address the goals of the learning tasks and provide evidence of student learning and progress over time.

- *Teacher-Made Tests:* Forced choice or open response items used to show understanding of concepts or application of skills. Examples include multiple-choice items; questions requiring explanations, drawings, etcetera; and the writing of letters or essays.

- *Products or Projects:* Student constructions including designs, inventions, models, organized research and information gathering, demonstrations of knowledge or skill, community investigations, etcetera. Products should include communication to show student thinking as well as self-assessment about learning and new questions.

- *Performance Tasks:* A series of tasks, or a single multistep task, that allows students to demonstrate understanding of concepts, ability to perform skills, habits of mind and dispositions, and the ability to make connections to related issues. Students generate responses through writing, collecting data and drawing conclusions, applying what they learned, drawing, graphing, etcetera.

- *Folios and Portfolios:* Samples of student work kept in an organized manner. May show growth over time; samples can be self-selected by students or teacher selected; students can annotate work samples by describing what makes the work noteworthy.

- *Criterion-Referenced Tests and Quizzes:* Sets of questions that relate directly to the context in which concepts, skills, etcetera. have been learned. Scores are interpreted by checking mastery.

- *Norm-Referenced Tests:* A set of questions covering a wide range of content in order to distribute student responses along a normal curve.

USING MULTIPLE AND VARIED ASSESSMENTS

The varied assessments are like lenses through which student learning is viewed. Some assessments provide only one type of evidence of learning while others, such as performance assessments, are able to capture evidence of learning of several instructional goals. In order to obtain a comprehensive picture of student achievement, multiple and varied assessments must be used throughout the instructional unit. Frequent assessment not only monitors student achievement, but it can also be used to inform and guide the instructional process.

Figure 8.1 shows a chart with the assessment tools, the types of evidence of student learning that can be obtained through the assessment tool, and one or more examples.

Figure 8.1   Types of Assessments, Type of Evidence of Learning, and Examples

Type of Assessment	Type of Evidence Captured	Examples
Observation Checklist	Dispositions, behaviors	Ability to work well in a cooperative learning group, respect for equipment, willingness to share ideas and help colleagues
	Completion of tasks	Checklist of things to do
Interviews and Dialogue	Understanding of directions, description of procedures, explanations of findings and data, concept understanding, connections, new questions	While students are engaged in activity, teacher visits groups and informally asks questions. Teacher asks for clarification of written work or data, examples or meaning
Learning Logs or Notebooks	Written descriptions of components of investigation, data and conclusions, rationale and thinking process	Notebooks with entries
Teacher-Made Tests	Vocabulary and concept understanding, relationships between concepts, meaning and applications of concepts	Items may be forced choice or open response questions to show understanding, may include drawings and references to data, questions requiring explanations of meaning and applications
Products and Projects	Ability to access and use new information purposefully, ability to design or develop product that relates to a key concept, shows creativity, ability to make applications, problem-solving skills	Brochures or posters, research reports, inventions, challenges, new solutions to problems, technological designs
Performance Tasks	Ability to apply learning to new problem, understanding of concepts, use of process and thinking skills, logical reasoning	Tasks that require concept applications or that introduce problems and ask for creative solutions based on learning
Portfolios	Student work that shows concept understanding and/or skill development	Samples of best work, test papers, projects and products, self-assessments of work and learning
Criterion-Referenced Tests and Norm-Referenced Tests	Concept understanding related to state and national goals and standards, content knowledge	NAEP, SAT, ACT California/Iowa Tests of Basic Skills

Thought and Discussion

1. Give examples of ways that you have used one or more of the assessment strategies to determine if instructional goals were met.

2. Select one activity from this book. Identify a variety of ways the key concepts and skills addressed in the activity might be assessed using the components of the Assessment Tool Kit.

3. What assessment strategies provide diagnostic information? How can that information be used to guide instruction?

4. Identify assessment strategies that you would like to know more about.

Revisit the Initial Question

In what ways does inquiry-based science allow students to show what they know and are able to do?

Using the Eight Essentials to Enhance Learning

9

In summary, scientific inquiry refers to the diverse ways in which scientists study the natural world and propose explanations based on the evidence derived from their work. In schools, it refers to the activities of students by which they develop knowledge and understanding of scientific ideas and of how scientists study the natural world (National Research Council, 1996, p. 23).

Inquiry requires identification of assumptions, use of critical and logical thinking, and consideration of alternative explanations. Components of successful scientific inquiry include:

- prior establishment of an adequate knowledge base
- student reflection on concepts that guide inquiry
- examination of student misconceptions
- use of skills to analyze evidence and data
- ability to make connections between evidence and explanations
- use of science concepts in conversation and explanations

Eight Essentials addresses factors that need to be considered when making decisions about what to teach and how to teach to meet the goals of a standards-based science curriculum. The vision for science education includes a student-centered, inquiry-based approach to teaching and learning. The Eight Essentials provide an operational definition for this vision of effective inquiry that captures the essence of the discipline by addressing standards and key concepts, skills, and dispositions, and by providing a blueprint for developing and implementing high quality instructional materials. The degree to which curriculum materials and classroom practices match the definition of effective inquiry will vary, but the Eight Essentials provide a set of criteria against which to measure curriculum materials and classroom practices.

EIGHT-POINT LESSONS

The Eight Essentials may be used as a framework for the design and development of integrated instructional units and activities. The examples presented here show some of the ways that the Essentials may be embedded into instructional units and activities. Not every instructional activity will address all Eight Essentials; however, care should be taken to include all Eight Essentials within an instructional unit.

It is important that instructional activities are designed and developed or modified to meet specific state, school district, school, and classroom instructional standards and goals and that the activities provide meaningful learning experiences for students.

SAMPLE #1 GRADE LEVELS K–4: WHAT IS A BUTTERFLY?

This activity is part of a unit dealing with the life cycle of insects. Butterflies are beautiful organisms that young children find fascinating and exciting. Students will be introduced to butterflies and their body parts to familiarize them with insects in general, and with butterflies in particular. They will investigate models and pictures or living organisms to discover their body parts, and they will compare structures and their functions to their own body structures and functions. They will compare the adult form of the butterfly to the other forms as they study the stages in the life cycle of the butterfly and note the changes that occur throughout the cycle. Additional studies of the form and function of the adult butterfly should follow as each individual stage in the life cycle is studied in detail.

Unit Content Goals (Essential #1)

National Standard—*Characteristics of Organisms*

- Organisms have basic needs. For example, animals need air, water, and food.
- Each animal has different structures that serve different functions in growth, survival, and reproduction.
- The behavior of individual organisms is influenced by internal cues.

National Standard—*Life Cycles of Organisms*

- Animals have life cycles that include being born, developing into adults, reproducing, and eventually dying. The details of this life cycle are different for different organisms.

Instructional Objectives (Essentials #1 and #2)

1. Students will make observations and describe the three body parts (head, thorax, and abdomen) and physical properties of butterflies—head with eyes, antennae, and proboscis; wings with an array of patterns; and six legs.

2. Students will describe the ways insect body parts compare to human body parts.

3. Students will make inferences about the functions of body parts and conduct research or additional observations (following the emergence of butterflies during the life cycle) to determine their functions.

Background Information

The butterfly's body is complex and well adapted for survival. Like the bodies of all insects, the butterfly's body is divided into three parts: the *head*, the *thorax*, and the *abdomen*.

The *head* has a pair of antennae that are used for both touch and smell. A pair of large, round compound eyes are able to see color. Together, the eyes and antennae give the butterfly the ability to find food, to recognize a potential mate, and to select plant material on which to lay eggs. The long mouth tube, the proboscis, remains coiled when not in use. When uncoiled, it is nearly as long as the adult's body and can reach into the deep recesses of a flower to reach nectar.

The *thorax* is the midsection that holds both the two pairs of wings and the three pairs of jointed legs. Besides enabling the butterfly to fly, the wings often display a distinctive pattern that can be recognized by others of its kind. Wings protect the butterfly by giving it a way to escape predators and by camouflaging it. The two sides of the wings often have different colors and different patterns. The butterfly, like all insects, has six jointed legs. Butterflies taste with their second and third pairs of feet.

The *abdomen* houses the sex organs at the tip and is more rounded in females. The abdomen is relatively soft and is divided into segments. The abdomen contains the butterfly's flexible, tube-like heart, reproductive organs, breathing spores, and most of the digestive system.

Additional information on hundreds of species of butterflies in the United States and Mexico, including distribution maps, checklists, etcetera, can be found at:

- The butterflies page of the Northern Prairie Wildlife Research Center: http://www.npwrc.usgs.gov/resource/distr/lepid/bflyusa/bflyusa.htm
- *Butterflies at Zoom School*, which is all about butterflies, their anatomy, life cycles and reproduction, diet, senses, defense mechanisms, flying, etcetera: http://www.enchantedlearning.com/subjects/butterfly/
- A Web site about the biology and ecology of butterflies and moths: http://www.butterflies-moths.com/

Materials

An assortment of models of butterflies, preserved specimens, live butterflies, or pictures of butterflies; magnifiers; a variety of reference books and trade books; student notebooks.

Procedures

Engagement (Essential #3)

Ask students if they have ever observed butterflies outdoors and allow them to share their experiences and understanding of these organisms. Identify interests and misconceptions.

Ideas for Engagement:

Show students pictures of butterflies and ask them to describe the characteristics they see. In what ways are the butterflies alike? In what ways are they different?

Read a short book about butterflies to add interest, but the story should not tell about changes during the life cycle, which students will discover through investigation.

Allow students to observe one or more butterflies in captivity (could be the adults from another class's study of the life cycle before they are released), mounted specimens, or models. During the exploration stage, they will study the structure of these amazing insects in detail.

Ask students what they know about a nursery. Let them know they are going to establish a "butterfly nursery" to learn how these unique organisms go through several stages before they emerge as the beautiful adults they see.

Ask students what they would like to know about butterflies. Whenever possible, set up opportunities for students to be able to answer their questions throughout the study.

Exploration (Essentials #2, #6, and #7)

Introduce the inquiry questions: What is the structure of the adult butterfly? In what ways is the butterfly's structure similar to and different from yours?

1. Students should use notebooks for recording their questions, inquiry questions, and drawings.

2. Allow students time to observe butterflies and draw them. During the observation period, direct student attention to the body parts and, if live specimens are observed, how each body part is used.

3. Provide students the names for the three body parts they draw or have them research through available references: the head, the thorax, and the abdomen.

4. As students draw additional features, such as the eyes, proboscis, antennae, and wings, they should refer to pictures and diagrams for names and label their drawings.

5. Have students count the legs and include them in the drawing.

6. Students should record any other observations they make related to form and function in their notebooks. In addition, they should add inquiry questions.

Explanation (Essential #5)

Engage students in a discussion of their findings.

1. What are the three main parts of the butterfly's body?

2. What structures did you observe in the head? What function do you think they serve?

3. Describe the wings—number, shape, size, color, and other properties. What do the wings enable the butterfly to do?

4. How many legs are there? What is the function of these structures?

5. Use a Venn diagram to identify similarities and differences between butterfly structures and human (comparable) structures. Use the features: head, thorax, abdomen, wings, legs, eyes, proboscis, and antennae. Allow students to work with a partner to complete the diagram and explain their schemes. There is no one right diagram; what is most important is that students give logical reasons for their classification systems.

Figure 9.1   Venn Diagram Comparing Butterflies to Humans

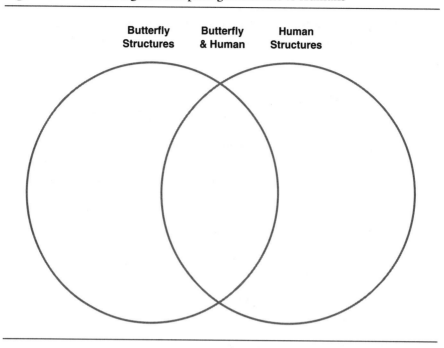

6. After students study the adult forms (after they study the egg, larva, and pupa stages), they may revisit their diagrams and modify them using new information.

Elaboration and Extensions (Essentials #4 and #5)

1. Students might study the symmetry of the butterfly and make a three-dimensional model of a butterfly showing the symmetry.

2. Students may study a particular type of butterfly, perhaps one that is native to the area in which they live. They may learn about the butterfly's habitat, needs for food and shelter, migration patterns, and other details of interest.

3. Discuss with students: Of what value are butterflies to the environment? What purposes do they serve?

A well-developed unit of instruction on butterflies will address the Essentials to a greater extent and include such things as a vocabulary list, additional background information, resources, references, and well-developed hands-on activities that address each of the stages in the life cycle of the insect: egg, larva, pupa (chrysalis), and adult. Students should study each stage as they make detailed drawings of the organism in their notebooks. They should note changes that the organism undergoes throughout its life cycle. Activities should address the needs of the animal at various stages of its life cycle. Comparisons should be made between complete metamorphosis and incomplete metamorphosis by comparing the life cycle of the butterfly to the life cycle of other organisms such as a grasshopper.

Evaluation (Essential #8)

Students should display their labeled drawings and be able to explain that butterflies are insects and describe the major body parts. Using their diagrams, they should describe some similarities and differences between insects and humans.

Students should describe the stages in the life cycle of the butterfly and the changes that occur throughout the cycle.

SAMPLE #2 GRADE LEVELS 5–8: TRANSFER OF ENERGY—INVESTIGATING HEAT

These two investigations lend themselves well to student-constructed inquiries where students design tests to answer the inquiry question, make observations, access information, plan and carry out the investigations, collect and display data, use tools and technology to analyze and interpret data, propose explanations, and communicate their findings. All phases of their work should be recorded in a notebook.

The procedures are shown for guided inquiry with components of the Eight Essentials identified.

Overview

The big idea of energy can be studied through life, earth, and physical science topics. In this activity students will learn about thermal equilibrium. In Part A, students will investigate the transfer of heat energy through water. They will observe and record the change in temperature that occurs when equal amounts of hot and cold water are mixed. In Part B, students will investigate the loss of heat from water over time. They will create a graph of their data and extrapolate as a way to predict future change.

The activities may be used as part of a unit on energy or heat energy (thermodynamics) or may be included in a unit on weather and factors that influence climate.

Unit Content Goals (Essential #1)

National Standards:

- Energy is a property of many substances and is associated with heat, light, electricity, mechanical motion, sound, nuclei, and the nature of a chemical.
- Energy is transferred in many ways.
- Heat moves in predictable ways, flowing from warmer objects to cooler ones, until both reach the same temperature.

Instructional Objectives and Goals (Essentials #1 and #2)

1. Students will explain the movement of heat from an area of greater concentration to one of lesser concentration.

2. Students will explain that when hot water is mixed with cool water, the warm water loses heat and the cool water gains heat until all the water is at the same temperature.

3. Students will describe their findings when investigating the loss of heat from water over time. They will collect and record data and create a graph of their data. They will explain how graphs can be used to show the relationship between two variables and plausible predictions.

Background Information

Thermodynamics is a branch of physics that deals with the energy and work of a system. Thermodynamics deals only with the large-scale response of a system that we can observe and measure in experiments.

Thermal Equilibrium

It is observed that a higher temperature object that is in contact with a lower temperature object will transfer heat to the lower temperature object. The objects will approach the same temperature, and in the absence of loss to or gain from other objects, they will then maintain a constant temperature. They are then said to be in *thermal equilibrium*. Objects in thermal equilibrium have the same temperature.

The heat energy of a substance is determined by how active its atoms and molecules are. An object or substance is hot when its atoms and molecules are excited and show rapid movement. In cooler objects or substances, molecules and atoms will be less excited and show less movement.

In the excited state, atoms and molecules take up a lot of space because they're moving around so fast. When atoms and molecules settle down, or cool down, they take up less space.

If a high energy atom comes into contact with a low energy atom, the excited atom will loose some of its energy to the cool atom. The two atoms will settle into an energy level that's between their starting points. The level at which they settle is thermal equilibrium. The details of the process of reaching thermal equilibrium are described in the first and second laws of thermodynamics.

Materials

Student thermometers in degrees Celsius or in Celsius and Fahrenheit; beakers with milliliter markings or plain beakers or cups and a graduated cylinder; source for cold water; hot plate or source of hot water (approximately 40 degrees Celsius or 100 degrees Fahrenheit); design a notebook page for the activity or have students add information as they work through the activity. See notebook components in Chapter 6.

Safety

Care must be taken when heating, pouring, and measuring hot water. Protective goggles for teachers and students and potholders or gloves should be used, or teachers should handle the hot liquid with students identifying the appropriate level on the beaker.

Procedures

Engagement (Essential #3)

Ask students if they have ever gone swimming in a lake and observed that the water is generally colder as they go deeper into the lake. The same phenomenon might have been observed when swimming in a large pool. What is the source of heat for lake water? If the sun warms the water at the surface of the lake, how does water under the surface get warm? Identify questions students have about the circulation of water and misconceptions they have.

Ideas for Engagement

In a unit of instruction dealing with water, students might be invited to assist scientists working in a hydrology lab where they will be testing water for various properties.

Other introductions may focus on applications of the principle. For example, race car drivers allow their engines to cool down while idling before shutting them down after a hard race. They do this to let all of the internal engine parts reach thermal equilibrium. The principle of thermal equilibrium will be investigated in Part A using water. The rate of heat loss over time for water will be investigated in Part B.

Exploration (Essentials #2, #6, and #7)

Part A:

Inquiry Question: What will happen to the temperatures of hot water and cold water when the two are mixed together?

1. Measure 200 milliliters of cold water into one beaker (A) and 200 milliliters of hot water into a second beaker (B). Using a thermometer, measure the temperature of the water in each beaker in degrees Celsius. Record temperatures on the data table (Table 9.1).

2. Predict what the temperature of the water would be if the contents of beaker A were poured into beaker B.

3. Pour the contents of beaker A into beaker B and stir. Measure and record the temperature of the mixture of water.

4. Discuss: Did the water from beaker A gain or lose heat? Explain.

5. Did the water in beaker B gain or lose heat? Explain.

6. Write a summary statement about what happens to molecules of hot and cold water when they are mixed together.

Table 9.1   Data Table for Temperature

	Water in Beaker A	*Water in Beaker B*	*Prediction for A + B*	*Water in A + B*
Temperature in Degrees C				

Part B:

Inquiry Question: At what rate will the temperature of hot water decrease over time?

1. Most students know from experience that water loses heat over time. Have them predict what they think the rate of decrease will be for a beaker of hot water.

2. Measure 200 milliliters of hot water into a beaker. Measure the temperature of the water in degrees Celsius and record it on the data table.

Figure 9.2   Graph for Change in Temperature

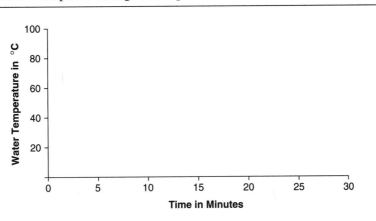

3. Predict what the temperature of the water will be after five minutes.

4. Measure the temperature of the water after five minutes and record.

5. Based on what you learned, predict the temperature of the water after another five minutes (at 10 minutes). Measure and record.

6. Measure and record temperatures after 15 minutes and 20 minutes.

7. Make a graph to show the change in water temperature over 20 minutes.

Table 9.2   Data Table for Temperature Over Time

	Starting Temperature	*Prediction 5 minutes*	*Temperature 5 minutes*	*Prediction 10 minutes*	*Temperature 10 minutes*	*Temperature 15 minutes*	*Temperature 20 minutes*
Temperature in Degrees C							

Explanation (Essential #5)

1. Explain what happened to the temperature of water over time.

2. What was the rate of decrease after five minutes? After 10 minutes? After 20 minutes?

3. Was the rate of heat loss consistent? Explain.

4. Extend your line (use a dotted line) to show what the temperature will probably be after 30 minutes (extrapolate).

Elaboration and Extensions (Essentials #4 and #5)

1. Review what is meant by *thermal equilibrium*. At what temperature would water left in the open container reach thermal equilibrium?

2. Learn more about electric heat and the role of electricity in producing heat in such things as toasters and hair dryers. Learn about the movement of heat in refrigerators, heat engines, automobile cooling systems, air conditioners, and heat pumps.

3. What are the trade-offs (environmental, financial, or risks) associated with the generation of electricity? Write a summary of the trade-offs associated with the generation of electricity.

(Lesson modified from PowerMasters Motorsports Academy; Lesson on Heat Energy, http://www.powermasters.com/heat_energy.html)

Evaluation (Essential #8)

1. Students will explain thermal equilibrium as the movement of heat from an area of greater concentration to lesser concentration.

2. Students will explain how thermal equilibrium was reached when hot water was mixed with cold water and support their conclusion with their data.

3. Students will describe the rate at which water loses heat over time and support their conclusions with data.

4. Students will explain how graphs can be used to show the relationship between two variables and plausible predictions through extrapolation.

USING THE EIGHT ESSENTIALS TO ANALYZE CURRICULUM MATERIALS

High quality classroom instruction associated with well-designed and executed instructional materials meets the diverse needs of students and promotes student achievement. High quality instruction can best be accomplished when teachers have access to instructional programs and materials that are rich with opportunities to address the Eight Essentials.

Figure 9.3 Analysis of Curriculum Materials for the Eight Essentials

Title: _____

Inquiry-based Science . . .	Way(s) Addressed in the Materials	Comments, Recommendations, & Suggestions
1. Develops an understanding of basic concepts		
2. Develops process & thinking skills		
3. Actively engages students in a learning cycle		
4. Builds understanding of ways that science is linked to technology & society		
5. Provides experience necessary to support & develop or modify interpretations of the world		
6. Enhances reading & writing		
7. Allows for a diversity of strategies for learning		
8. Allows for a variety of ways for students to show what they know and are able to do		

The inventory in Figure 9.3 can be used to analyze individual instructional activities and programs for the ways they address each of the Eight Essentials of inquiry-based science.

New insights about quality instruction will develop through practice and discussion. For each of the Eight Essentials, you can write comments, recommendations, or suggestions for improving or enhancing the activity or program, as needed.

Questions for Discussion

1. Discuss your analysis of activities or programs. Which components of inquiry are addressed well? Which components are not addressed well?

2. What is missing from the activity, unit, or program that needs to be there to address the goals and standards of the curriculum?

3. What are some ways the weak areas can be strengthened?

4. What do we need to know or research to further develop and enhance the instructional program?

5. How will the proposed changes help promote high quality teaching and learning in the classroom?

References

Abraham, M. R. (1997, January 7). The learning cycle approach to science instruction. *Research Matters—To the Science Teacher*, No. 9701. Retrieved March 10, 2005, from http://www.educ.sfu.ca/narstsite/publications/ research/cycle.htm

AIMS Education Foundation. (1987). *The sky's the limit*. Fresno, CA: Author.

AIMS Education Foundation. (1993). *Machine shop*. Fresno, CA: Author.

American Association for the Advancement of Science (AAAS). (1990). *Science for all Americans*. New York: Oxford University Press.

American Association for the Advancement of Science (AAAS). (1993). *Project 2061: Benchmarks for science literacy*. New York: Oxford University Press.

Anderson, R. D. (2002). Reforming science teaching: What research says about inquiry. *Journal of Science Teacher Education, 13*(1), 1–12.

Armstrong, T. (1998). *Awakening genius in the classroom*. Alexandria, VA: Association for Supervision and Curriculum Development.

Armstrong, T. (2003). *The multiple intelligences of reading and writing*. Alexandria, VA: Association for Supervision and Curriculum Development.

Baylor, B. (1978). *The other way to listen*. New York: Macmillan.

Beisty, S. (1992). *Incredible cross sections*. New York: Knopf.

Bellanca, J. (1995). *Designing professional development for change*. Arlington Heights, IL: IRI-SkyLight Training and Publishing.

Ben-Hur, M. (1998). Mediation of cognitive competencies for students in need. *Phi Delta Kappan, 79*(9), 661–666.

Birman, B. F., Desimone, L., Porter, A. D., & Garet, M. S. (2000). Designing professional development that works. *Educational Leadership, 58*(9), 28–32.

Black, P., & Wiliam, D. (1998). Inside the black box: Raising standards through classroom assessment. *Phi Delta Kappan, 79*(2), 139–148.

Blair, J. (2000). How teaching matters: Bringing the classroom back into discussion of teacher quality. *Education Week, 20*(8), 24.

Brophy, J. (1986). Teacher influences on student achievement. *American Psychologist, 41*(10), 1067–1077.

Bybee, R. W. (2002). *Learning science and the science of learning*, Alexandria, VA: National Science Teachers Association Press.

Caine, R. N., & Caine, G. (1991). *Teaching and the human brain*. Alexandria, VA: Association for Supervision and Curriculum Development.

Caine, R. N., & Caine, G. (1997). *Education on the edge of possibility.* Alexandria, VA: Association for Supervision and Curriculum Development.

Carle, E. (1992). *The very quiet cricket.* New York: Philomel Books.

Carson, R. (2002). *Silent spring.* NY: Houghton Mifflin. (Original work published 1962).

Committee on Education. (2004). *Lost in space: Science education in New York City public schools.* New York: Council of the City of New York

Csikszentmihalyi, M. (1990). *The psychology of optimal experience.* New York: HarperCollins.

Csikszentmihalyi, M. (1993). *The evolving self.* New York: HarperCollins.

Darling-Hammond, L. (1997). *The right to learn: A blueprint for creating schools that work.* San Francisco: Jossey-Bass.

Darling-Hammond, L., & McLaughlin, M. (1995). Policies that support professional development in an era of reform. *Phi Delta Kappan, 76*(8), 597–604.

DeHart Hurd, P. (1997). *Inventing science education for the new millennium.* New York: Teachers College Press.

Donovan, M. S., & Bransford, J. D. (Eds.). (2005). *How students learn: Science in the classroom.* Washington, DC: National Academies Press.

Eisenkraft, A. (2003). Expanding the 5E model. *Science Teacher, 70*(6), 56–59.

English, F. W. (1992). *Deciding what to teach and test.* Thousand Oaks, CA: Corwin.

Gabel, D. (1993). *Introductory science skills.* Prospect Heights, IL: Waveland Press.

Gardner, H. (1983). *Frames of mind: The theory of multiple intelligences.* New York: Basic Books.

Gardner, H. (1993). *Multiple intelligences: The theory in practice,* New York: Basic Books.

Gardner, H. (1999). *Intelligence reframed: Multiple intelligences for the 21st century.* New York: Basic Books.

Gartrell, J. E. (1989). *Methods of motion: An introduction to mechanics.* Alexandria, VA: National Science Teachers Association.

Gartrell, J. E., & Schafer, L. E. (1990). *Evidence of energy: An introduction to mechanics.* Alexandria, VA: National Science Teachers Association.

Golman, D. (1995). *Emotional intelligence.* New York: Bantam Books.

Gossett, C. S., et al. (2000). *Sense-able science.* Fresno, CA: AIMS Education Foundation.

Greenhouse effect . . . (n.d.). Retrieved March 4, 2005, from www.epa.gov/globalwarming/kids/greenhouse.html

Gregory, G. H., & Chapman, C. (2002). *Differentiated instructional strategies: One size doesn't fit all.* Thousand Oaks, CA: Corwin.

Guskey, T. R. (2000). *Evaluating professional development.* Thousand Oaks, CA: Corwin.

Hammerman, E., & Musial, D. (1995). *Classroom 2061: Activity-based assessments in science.* Arlington Heights, IL: SkyLight Training and Publishing.

Hann, J. (1991). *How science works.* Pleasantville, NY: Reader's Digest Association.

Harvard-Smithsonian Center for Astrophysics. (1987). *Private universe.* Burlington, VT: Annenberg/CPB Math and Science Collection.

Hazen, R. M., & Trefil, J. (1991) *Science matters.* New York: Doubleday.

Hewitt, P. (1989). *Conceptual physics.* Glenview, IL: Scott Foresman.

Hofstadter, D., & Fluid Analogies Research Group. (1995). *Fluid concepts and creative analogies: Computer models of the fundamental mechanisms of thought.* New York: Basic Books.

Holloway, J. (2000). How does the brain learn science? *Educational Leadership, 58*(3), 85–86.

Hosking, W. (1990). *Flights of imagination.* Alexandria, VA: National Science Teachers Association.

Jensen, E. (1998). *Teaching with the brain in mind.* Alexandria, VA: Association for Supervision and Curriculum Development.

Jensen, E. (2000). *Brain-based learning.* San Diego, CA: Brain Store.

Joyce, B., & Showers, B. (1995). *Student achievement through staff development.* New York: Longman.

Klein, L. (Executive Producer). (2000). *Building big.* [Television series]. Boston: WGBH.

Klentschy, M., Garrison, L., & Maia Amaral, O. (2000). *Valle imperial project in science (VIPS): Four-year comparison of student achievement data, 1995–1999.* El Centro, CA: El Centro School District.

Lapp, D. (2001). Bridging the gaps. *Science Link, 12*(1), 1–2.

Lichen blamed for mystery elk deaths. (2004, March 23). [Electronic version]. *Billings Gazette.* Retrieved March 10, 2005, from http://www.billingsgazette .com/index.php?ts=1&display=rednews/2004/03/23/build/wyoming/ 30-lichens-elkdeaths

Lieberman, A. (1995). Practices that support teacher development. *Phi Delta Kappan, 76*(8), 591–696.

Liem, T. L. (1987). *Invitations to science inquiry.* Lexington, MA: Ginn Press.

Loucks-Horsley, S, P., Hewson, W., Love, N., & Stiles, K. E. (1998). *Designing professional development for teachers of science and mathematics.* Thousand Oaks, CA: Corwin.

Macaulay, D. (1988). *The way things work.* Boston: Houghton Mifflin.

Macaulay, D. (2000). *Building big.* Boston: Houghton Mifflin.

Marzano, R. J. (1991). Fostering thinking across the curriculum through knowledge restructuring. *Journal of Reading, 34*(7), 518–525.

Marzano, R. J., Pickering, D. J., & Pollock, J. E. (2001). *Classroom instruction that works.* Alexandria, VA: Association for Supervision and Curriculum Development.

McBer, H. (2000). *Research into teacher effectiveness: A model of teacher effectiveness.* (Research Report #216). London: Department of Education and Employment.

McCormack, A. (1981). *Inventor's workshop.* Carthage, IL: Fearon Teacher Aids.

Moncure, J. B. (1990). *The five senses.* Elgin, IL: Child's World.

Moncure, J. B. (1990) *Life cycles,* Elgin, IL: Child's World.

Musial, D., & Hammerman, E. (1992). Framing knowledge through moments: A model for teaching thinking in science. *Teaching Thinking and Problem Solving, 14*(2), 12–15.

Musial, D., & Hammerman, E. (1997). *Framing ways of knowing in problem-based learning.* Unpublished manuscript.

National Commission on Mathematics and Science Teaching for the 21st Century. (2000). *Before it's too late.* Washington, DC: Author.

National Research Council. (1996). *National science education standards.* Washington, DC: National Academy Press.

National Research Council. (2000). *How people learn.* Washington, DC: National Academy Press.

National Science Resources Center. (1997). *Science for all.* Washington, DC: National Academy Press.

Peart, N. A., & Campbell, F. A. (1999). At-risk students' perception of teacher effectiveness. *Journal for a Just and Caring Education, 5*(3) 269–284.

Prelutsky, J. (1984). *The new kid on the block.* New York: Greenwillow Books.

Resnick, M. (2003). Playful learning and creative societies [Electronic version]. *Education Update, 8*(6).

Rowan, B., Chiang, F., & Miller, R. (1997). Using research in employees' performance to study the effects of teachers on students' achievement. *Sociology of Education, 70,* 256–284.

Samples, B., Hammond, B., & McCarthy, B. (1985). *4mat and science,* Barrington, IL: EXCEL, Inc.

Silver, H. F., Strong, R. W., & Perini, M. J. (2000). *So each may learn: Integrating learning styles and multiple intelligences.* Alexandria, VA: Association for Supervision and Curriculum Development.

Sparks, D., & Hirsh, S. (1997). *A new vision for staff development.* Alexandria, VA: Association for Supervision and Curriculum Development, and Oxford, OH: National Staff Development Council.

Stronge, J. H. (2002). *Qualities of effective teachers.* Alexandria, VA: Association for Supervision and Curriculum Development.

Sylwester, R. (1995). *A celebration of neurons.* Alexandria, VA: Association for Supervision and Curriculum Development.

Sylwester, R. (2000). *A biological brain in a cultural classroom.* Thousand Oaks, CA: Corwin.

Torp, L., & Sage, S. (1998). *Problems as possibilities.* Alexandria, VA. Association for Supervision and Curriculum Development.

U.S. Department of Energy Human Genome Program. (2003). *Genomics and its impact on science and society: The Human Genome Project and beyond.* Retrieved March 3, 2005, from http://www.ornl.gov/TechResources/Human_Genome/publicat/primer/index.html

Weiss, I. R., et al. (2003). *Looking inside the classroom: A study of K-12 mathematics and science education in the United States.* Chapel Hill, NC: Horizon Research.

Wolfe, P. (2001). *Brain matters.* Alexandria, VA. Association for Supervision and Curriculum Development.

Index

CORWIN PRESS

The Corwin Press logo—a raven striding across an open book—represents the union of courage and learning. Corwin Press is committed to improving education for all learners by publishing books and other professional development resources for those serving the field of PreK–12 education. By providing practical, hands-on materials, Corwin Press continues to carry out the promise of its motto: **"Helping Educators Do Their Work Better."**